How David Cameron Fixed the 2015 Election and Much Else,

How They Plan To Fix The Next Election and

How We Could Restore a Prosperous Representative Democracy In Britain

By George Tait Edwards MBE

With two jointly co-authored articles by Bryan Gould

Edited by Liam Christian Lloyd

This book is dedicated to the hope that a prosperous representative democracy can be re-created in the United Kingdom in the near future.

Contents

Prologue
Finding your way around in this book

Sixteen of the 29 sections in this book have been previously published. The locations and dates of publication of these previously published items - one excerpt from a book, nine articles and one lecture - are stated at the beginning of each section. There are thirteen new sections in this book which have not been published elsewhere.

The numbering system within previously published articles has been reproduced and relocated in this book and to ensure the reader will know the article name and page number within the article or lecture, and these are given at the top right hand header on each page. (Eg "Prologue" in the Header at the top right hand side of this page.)

I have followed my usual practice of providing a purpose and outline of the book in Chapter 2 to enable rapid navigation to the subjects in which the reader may be interested. Section 2.2, the outline of the book, provides a one sentence summary of the purpose of each section of the book.

I have tried to use parliamentary language throughout this book, because no purpose is served by name-calling major politicians, whose actions speak much louder than their words.

In my considered opinion, if politicians are judged by the results of their actions you will never do them wrong. Politicians naturally try to find some noble aim to cloak their most objectionable activities. The blame for poor outcomes is often placed by politicians and the media upon the victims of government action rather than more accurately upon government politicians and their legislative activities. The responsibility for the results of government policies lies with these persons who have the power, with the politicians who have implemented damaging polices from allegedly high motives which are often just a camouflage for basic and often base partisan interests.

Nowhere is that observation more relevant than in the implementation of the *2013 Individual Elector Registration and Administration Act* which is a major subject of this book.

Often the framework of the economic policy of Western governments appears to be determined by a cultural-wide set of economic assumptions. The assumption of neoclassical economics is usually quoted and lies at the root of many malignant acts by the Anglosphere governments. That needs to change.

When China arrived at a late rapprochement with Japan and, after some Nixon-inspired "ping pong diplomacy", officially ended the discord of the Second World War on 25 September 1972, a new era in China's history began. The Chinese sent delegation after delegation into Tokyo to discover precisely how the Japanese had grown so rapidly since 1945, with a view to replicating Japan's high growth rates in China, which they did. The economists and politicians of the West did not do that, because they mistakenly thought they already had all the answers.

The Chinese discovered Shimomuran economics, the economic system explained by Dr Osamu Shimomura (1910-89) and practised by Japan from 1945-74. In *China's First Dictionary of Japanese History* and in the review of that book at http://www.chinajapan.org/articles/06.1/06.1tao13-18.pdf only one Japanese economist is given a towering importance. That review says

"The prominent economist Shimomura Osamu's (1910-89) career and theories (which became the basis for the Ikeda Cabinet's famous income-doubling plan) are detailed in two separate entries (pp. 46-47)"

There is no similar entry in Encyclopaedia Brittanica nor in any of the Western-produced books about Japanese economic history with few exceptions: seven of these are the books I have co-authored or written about economics (including this one, and see Appendix 2, where the six others are listed and the eighth is Professor Richard Werner's seminal book *new paradigm in macroeconomics* (Palgrove Macmillan, 2005) where Shimomura is mentioned on page 66.

In my opinion it is essential that the voters disenfranchised by the 2013 IER Act should re-register as voters as soon as possible. When a non-Conservative Government is elected, it is essential that it knows about the creative and competent Shimomuran-Wernerian macroeconomics practised in the Tokyo Consensus economies.

Hence the emphasis on, and the lengthy explanations of, that subject in this book.

The most disappointing aspect of Cameron's Conservative Government is that it offers neither a positive vision nor any progressive policies for the future of the United Kingdom. The destruction of the welfare state and the NHS leads nowhere. Austerity is a downward spiral into the destruction of much that is good in the United Kingdom, and gerrymandering offers no solution to continual economic decline, because the gerrymandering party have no idea about how to run a modern economy.

Yet a fully functioning representative democracy could be recreated in the United Kingdom, and particularly in England and Wales. It may be difficult to reverse the Cameron-led gerrymandering of the electoral rolls, but it seems entirely possible. That gerrymandering rests upon the assumption of voter apathy and inaction and I think that situation will not continue.

We'll see.

1 Background

The main subject of this book is, as David Lindsay noted in an article published on the internet at on 7 October 2011, "the biggest political scandal you've never heard of" (see http://davidaslindsay.blogspot.co.uk/2011/10/great-gerrymander.html). This book explains how Thatcher in 1989 and 1990 and Cameron from 2012 passed and implemented various vexatious legislations to reduce deliberately the non-Conservative voters on the Parliamentary Electoral Rolls. These actions resulted in two general elections that set the pollsters on their ears. The first was the General Election of 1992 which elected the John Major Government against all the predictions of the pollsters. The second is the 7 May 2015 General Election which returned the extreme right wing Conservative Government of David Cameron.

At first sight these elections seem as if the pollsters simply got it wrong. But a more detailed examination demonstrates that the reason for both of these surprises was Conservative gerrymandering. Thatcher's Poll Tax reduction of non-conservative voters in Scotland from 1989 and in England and Wales from 1990 was instrumental in producing the 1992 John Major Government. The 2013 Individual Elector Registration and Administration Act, (often referred to in this book as the 2013 IER Act) again reduced non-conservative voters and produced the surprising Conservative victory in the General Election of 7 May 2015.

Much worse is to come. 7 million of the voters on current Parliamentary Rolls are currently being asked to provide further evidence of their identity - their place and date of birth and their National Insurance Number and signature - and if they do not respond by December 2015 these largely non-Conservative voters will be removed from the voting rolls.
The Conservative Party has decided to finalise the transition to the 2013 IER voting registers a year early in December 2015, and then lock in the lower numbers of voters through constituency boundary changes which may prevent any other party, apart from the Conservatives, from ever being elected again under the 2013 IER arrangements. These actions makes a large Conservative majority very likely. See http://www.telegraph.co.uk/news/11593496/New-

Commons-boundaries-top-Conservative-government-agenda.html
The 2013 IER Act makes the control of the Parliamentary Electoral
Roll effectively into a Government Department and the
implementation of that Act has been entirely partisan. Britain can no
longer be regarded as a fully representative democracy because a
significant non-Conservative minority has been deliberately
disenfranchised. It might be possible but it will be very difficult to
reverse that position. Most British people do not realise the basic
facts about this situation. This book is an attempt to provide these.
The major second subject of this book is about an alternative
macroeconomics, about how an incoming British Government could
adopt the economic system which has worked to well in the Tokyo
Consensus Zone. There is no need whatsoever for the continuation of
a malign and damaging austerity programme and this book sets out a
practical and workable alternative. Austerity leads nowhere, yet the
Cameron Government acts as if there is no available exit from
increasing austerity, but there is no need for that policy to be
practised if the government and its advisors had an adequate
economic understanding. Furthermore, the 2013 IER Act has
resulted in a Conservative Government which lacks democratic
legitimacy, which does not have any sound mandate to implement the
attacks on the poor, the reduction in the costs and size of
Government and the austerity programme which it pursues.

Finally this book touches upon how a fully functioning representative
democracy could be re-established in the UK and speculates upon the
future of David Cameron and his place in history as the greatest
British gerrymanderer.

2 Purposes and outline of this book

2.1 Purposes The primary purpose of this book is to set out, as meticulously as I can, the recent history and probable future of Conservative gerrymandering in the United Kingdom from the period from the late 1980s until about 2020. This period covers the past 27 years (roughly from Thatcher's Poll Tax Gerrymander set out in section 3.2 through the more minor gerrymander of the so-called "bedroom tax" and the major gerrymander of the 2013 Individual Electoral Registration (IER) Act and the next five years so as to include the more recent and major changes which are still underway.

A major secondary purpose of this book is to set out likely future effects. It appears to me that three of the so far unimplemented aspects of the 2013 IER Act - first, the requirement that 7m mainly non-Conservative voters justify their presence on the existing 2013 IER Act Parliamentary Electoral Roll by December 2015 or be removed from that roll, second the bringing forward of the end-date of the introduction of that Act from December 2016 to December 2015, and third the redrawing or gerrymandering of Parliamentary Constituency boundaries in 2016 to reduce the numbers of MPs from 650 to 600 or less - imply the future lock out of IER non-voters in its lower voter registration and threaten to make inadequate voter registration into a permanent fact of political history.

A third purpose of this book is to comment upon why the British media have neglected to comment upon the gerrymandering of the voters registers after the 7 May 2015 GE, and to speculate upon the reasons for that result.

A fourth purpose is to set out possible solutions for restoring a fully fledged democratic government in Britain, one of which was prefigured by the Chartists in 1842, and how a better economic understanding could produce a much better future for all the people of Britain. And a better future for all the people in the Anglosphere, especially Greece.

Fifth, I discuss the political, social and economic aspects of Cameron's programme for the future of Britain - the political implications of a Conservative Government which lacks a genuine democratic mandate, the social implications of the attack upon the living standards of the poor, often non-voters, and the dismantling of the Welfare State by a Government which lacks a fully democratic mandate to do that, and the lack of economic understanding about how to create more rapid economic growth which has dogged all British Governments since the mid-1880s.

In the conclusions I speculate on the future of David Cameron because as a gerrymandering Prime Minister he seems to lack both the essential democratic mandate and the necessary judgement to continue in his current position.

Finally in Appendix 1 I provide a key article about how more rapid economic growth could be arranged in any nation (the example refers to the UK, but the ten basic principles could be enacted in any country) and in Appendix 2 I provide a list of the two other books I have co-authored with John Carrington and the three books I have authored on my own, as well as references to the thirty-four articles published on the London Progressive Journal at http://londonprogressivejournal.com/user/view/2285, the ten articles co-authored with Bryan Gould at http://londonprogressivejournal.com/user/view/6214 and the fifty articles published at https://medium.com/me/stories/public.

2.2 Outline of this book

This book is organised into five main chapters. The headings of each chapter are the Background to this topic in Chapter 1, the Purposes and outline of the book in Chapter 2, the Evidence and comment about gerrymandering in Chapter3, The Future in Chapter 4, and Conclusions in Chapter 5.

The contents of the first Chapter ("Background") and second Chapter (Purposes and outline of the book) are self-explanatory from their headings.

The Third Chapter starts with a fresh summary (section 3.1) about the recent history of Conservative gerrymandering, which covers Thatcher's Poll Tax, the "Bedroom Tax", and the 2013 IER Tax.

In section 3.2 Thatcher's "Poll Tax" (referred to in the legislation as a "Community Charge") was a deliberate gerrymander, as all poll taxes have been, introduced in Scotland in 1989 and in England and Wales in 1990, and succeeded in its objective of producing a fourth Conservative victory in 1992.

Section 3.3 republishes the article first published on 4th May 2015, three days before the 7th May 2015 General Election, and asks "Is Britain now Too Gerrymandered To Be A Genuine Democracy?"

Section 3.4 republishes the 25 May 2015 article "A Gerrymandered Election and A Flawed Mandate" By Bryan Gould and George Tait Edwards.

Section 3.5 republished the 11th June 2015 article which asks the question "What if David Cameron is a Foolish Gerrymandering Politician?"

Section 3.6 discusses "Britain's Useless Media" which notes that the British media has generally ignored the burning question about how the Conservatives won the 2015 General Election.

In section 3.7 I suggest that the Conservative Government have no democratic mandate for the destruction of the British Social Contract or the NHS

In section 3.8 I republish 'Osborne's Dream of the Continuation of Neoclassical Economics

Is "A Boot Stamping On Human Face Forever"' By Bryan Gould and George Tait Edwards

Section 3.9 sets out "How the Cameron Government Stole the 2015 General Election - The Coalition and Conservative Implementation of the 2013 Individual Elector Registration Act"

Section 3.10 asks the question "Has David Cameron Committed Misconduct While in Public Office?" which seems likely to me, but a successful prosecution seems unlikely.

The Fourth Chapter discusses the possible futures of Britain given current circumstances.

Section 4.1 sets out Cameron's plan for a one-party state in the future of England.

Section 4.2 reproduces the article "A Tale of Two Prime Ministers" contrasting the policies of David Cameron the Neo-classical against Shinzo Abe the Shimomuran

Section 4.3 reproduces the article "The Alternative 2013 Spending Review, Or What Mr Osborne Could Have Said If He Understood Macro-economics"

Section 4.4 republishes the article "An Anti-Austerity 2015 UK Budget" which suggests how a better economic understanding can produce a much better set of policies and outcomes for the UK.

Section 4.5 points to the absence of economic alternatives to neoclassical macroeconomics in UK and Western Universities and suggests a greater freedom of thought is required if British universities are to provide a overdue improvement in macroeconomic thought.

Section 4.6 republishes the article "Shimomuran Economics is the Most Significant Advance Ever Made in Economic Understanding and the West Still Doesn't Get It" but I do hope someday they will.

Section 4.7 republishes my list of "Dr Osamu Shimomura's Major Achievements"

Section 4.8 reproduces provides the full text and slides of my 3 March 2015 Gresham College lecture called "The Curious Case of the Economist the West Forgot" along with the accompanying notes.

Section 4.9 reproduces the article about "How Japan Zoomed from War Devastation into Prosperity 1945-52" and presents the key information and comment about that event.

Section 4.10 suggests how a fully representative democracy in the United Kingdom could be re-established.

Chapter 5 presents my conclusions to this book.

In section 5.1 I discuss the future of David Cameron and speculate about his place in history and how soon he might go there.

In section 5.2 I talk around the proverb "Where there is no vision, the people perish" (proverbs 29:18) and suggest that a better vision and a deeper economic understanding for the British people could provide a much better future.

In Appendix 1 I republish an article called "How to Create an Economic Miracle in the UK or Elsewhere" which is not only relevant to the UK but also of general relevance to any political leader or group wishing to know how to maximise national economic growth with minimal inflation.
In Appendix 2 I list the six books and refer to the sources of the 18 media articles (1979-85) and 94 internet articles written or co-authored by me.

3 Evidence

3.1 The recent history of Conservative gerrymandering This Chapter sets out the history of Conservative gerrymandering in the UK - how Thatcher's 1989-1990 Poll Tax, the Under-occupancy penalty (or "Bedroom Tax" enshrined in the Reform Act 2012)) and the IER Act 2013, have all had the objective of chasing non-conservative voters off the Parliamentary Electoral Rolls so as to create an Conservative majority in subsequent elections.
A basic premise of this book is that politicians should not be judged on the basis of what they claim they are trying to do, they should be judged by their results. Politicians invariably cover their teeth with flowers and usually claim high and sometimes noble objectives, or a cost-saving objective, as a cover story for partisan and appalling real results. The outcomes of government actions are always more relevant and real than the claimed aims of government policy.

Thatcher's Poll Tax was justified as being a fairer method of replacing the rates. But the names of payers were taken from the Electoral Rolls and many previous voters decided they would rather give up the right to vote and de-register rather than pay the tax of about £400 a year to vote once every five years or so - a total of up to £2,000 per parliamentary vote per elector. That result is entirely in line with history. Poll taxes have never been about raising government revenues, they have always been about denying poor people the vote. Thatcher's Poll Tax was no exception to that general rule.

The Bedroom Tax at first glance looks eminently sensible as a "right-sizing" of housing need to provision - families receiving benefit are required to downsize into right-sized accommodation or face a 14% (for one "extra" bedroom) or 25% (for two "extra" bedrooms) housing benefit cut. But as reported in Wikipedia (see https:// en.wikipedia.org/wiki/Under-occupancy_penalty) and as quoted in that source and argued by the *Independent Newspaper* "96% of people that will be affected by the changes are not able to move [within their existing Local Authority] due to the lack of available social housing." And again from that Wikipedia reference "Two-thirds of individuals affected by the under-occupancy penalty are registered as disabled." The number of bedrooms in local authorities does not match the new need created by this Act, which is mainly an attack on the living standards of the disabled (who often need an extra room for an overnight carer and a wheelchair) and is producing the relocation of millions of voters who are local authority housing tenants, who are initially and maybe even in the long run less likely to re-register as voters. Whatever its declared intentions, the Bedroom Tax is an attack on the living standards and current location of the disabled, and a gerrymandering measure aimed at an ethic cleansing of poorer Council house voters from London (which is currently its main result).

The alleged objective of the 2013 IER Act is to remove the possibility of electoral fraud. But the method of implementation of that Act is to remove millions of voters from the Parliamentary electorate. There have been less than 10 successful prosecutions for electoral fraud during the last decade. The 2013 IER Act removes millions of mainly non-Conservative voters from the Parliamentary Electoral Rolls and has produced the "Surprise" of the 2015 GE Conservative victory. To deny the vote to millions of voters to prevent less than a dozen fraudulent votes demonstrates that this Act was, is, and always will be, a gerrymandering measure. David Lindsay saw it coming in the autumn of 2011 (see David Lindsay's blogspot at http://davidaslindsay.blogspot.co.uk/2011/10/great-gerrymander.html) and the Westminster opposition politicians tried in vain to make this change - which is the biggest change in voter registration since the general franchise - more representative by suggesting ways to increase voter registration. That didn't work. The Cameron-led Coalition Government voted for a partisan outcome at every stage in the implementation process of the 2013 IER Act.

3.2 17 December 2014 - "Thatcher's Poll Tax ("Community Charge") Gerrymander. Introduced in Scotland in 1989 and in England and Wales in 1990". As Wikipedia comments at https://en.wikipedia.org/wiki/Community_Charge,

"There is also some evidence that the poll tax had a lasting effect of people not registering themselves on the electoral register to evade collection attempts. This may have had an effect on the results of the 1992 general election, which ended in a fourth successive Conservative victory, despite most opinion polls pointing to a hung parliament or narrow Labour majority.[3]"

Below is a slightly edited excerpt from Section 7.10 of my 17 December 2014 book "Lucky bastards of the United Kingdom - The Story of the Economic Bomb" available at http://www.lulu.com/gb/en/shop/george-tait-edwards/lucky-bastards-of-the-20th-century/paperback/product-21958236.html This article was also published on the internet on June 15th 2015 at https://medium.com/@georgetaitedwards/thatcher-s-poll-tax-gerrymander-112ffe2e918e Please note that this excerpt from my sixth book is a fictionalised account of conversations held in the late 1980s. I wish the reader to understand fully some of the arguments about the Poll Tax before it was introduced and had then, and have now, no wish to embarrass friends living or dead who were usefully frank in their views. There is no such person as Clementine.

"'*The 24th Amendment (1964) to the Constitution of the United States reads:*
"*ABOLITION OF POLL TAXES*
Section 1: The right of citizens of the United States to vote in any primary or other election for President or Vice-President, for electors for President or Vice-President, or for senators or representative in Congress, shall not be denied or abridged by the United States or any state by reason of failure to pay the poll tax or any other tax.
Section 2: The Congress shall have power to enforce this article through appropriate legislation."
'When I met Clementine for lunch, he was exultant.
"We have got a really good system with the poll tax!" he told me.

"A flat head count tax on all adults over 18, unrelated to their ability to pay, has never seemed fair," I commented. "It is also not a good method of collecting tax."

"Who said it was just a method of collecting tax? That's not what it's meant to do! It will raise some taxes, sure, but that isn't its main purpose."

"What is it meant to do, then?" I asked

"Don't you know your history? What is the 24th Amendment to the Constitution of the United States? For the last two centuries, poll taxes have never been about tax collection. A poll tax is about denying poor people the vote. The tax is intended to chase the poorest voters off the electoral register, and since the poor mainly vote labour, that will create a few crucial percentage points in favour of the conservatives."

"You'll never get away with that!" I was appalled.

"Oh yes we will!! It will be the biggest and most successful gerrymandering ever done in this country. In the United States, it is illegal to deny the vote to those who have not paid their taxes. Fortunately this country does not have a written constitution, so there is nothing illegal about denying poor people the vote." He chuckled at the cunning of it all.

"Aren't we lucky bastards in the United Kingdom?" I asked ironically. "No written constitution, so the government can do as it likes!"

"Yes, we are lucky bastards," Clementine said in a measured way.

"Even if you do get away with it, it won't give you enough seats to matter!" I suggested. "It never surprises me that politicians behave badly, but I am always astonished they do so for such little advantage!"

"How many more seats does a 1% swing produce?" Clementine asked.

"One percent? Six seats?" I suggested.

"And you are the mathematician here," Clementine mocked me. "In a first-past-the-post system, the share of seats in parliament, if I remember right, is proportional to the third power of the fraction of the vote. So a 1% swing might produce a 10% increased or decreased share of seats. The conservatives may win the next election, and nobody will understand why!" Clementine was clearly more interested in giving me an appreciation of his party's cleverness, in the hope I might admire that, rather than a justification of its morality.

"Your party will never get away with it. The British press may not be much good, but they will see through this ruse. They will find out what you are doing," I said hopefully.

"They'll approve, the ones who understand it," said Clementine. "And they wouldn't oppose us anyway. All of the British press are our supporters! Their support is guaranteed, whatever we do."

"Not all the newspapers support the conservatives!"

"All of the important ones do!" he cried.

"That's another of your daft definitions. If I point out that say, the Guardian newspaper does not support the conservatives, or that the Independent is neutral, you will just say they are unimportant."

"Don't quibble—you know what I am saying is true. There are other advantages to this poll tax. The government wishes to control and reduce the incomes of local authorities, which are mainly left-wing anyway, but it isn't politically acceptable to do that openly. The poll tax will be so difficult to collect from the poor that the tax will act as an effective cut in income to the poorest boroughs in Britain. It will force a reduction in local authority activities and incomes where there is most poverty. The poorer they are, the more they lose! The poll tax will force left-wing local authorities into prosecuting the poor non-payers within their electorates, alienating their supporters by doing that and eroding their own power bases. What a neat system!"

"It sounds like another twist in the hellish downward spiral of British society."

"Now you know there's no such thing as society," Clementine joked with a smile.

"Isn't gerrymandering illegal?" I asked.

"It isn't if you don't get caught. And we will go on and on and on about how the poll tax is a fairer method of raising taxes. It's completely unworkable, of course, and the legislation will probably have to be repealed. But it will fix the next election for us, and it will be the devil's job for anybody ever to get the electoral register up to date again."

Clementine telephoned me about a week later to say that he had been joking.

"These things I said about the poll tax being a gerrymandering device

—they were not true!" he said. "I was only joking! I was surprised you took it so seriously! The poll tax really is a tax-raising device!" "I have checked what you told me," I advised him. "Your previous assertion is more convincing than this subsequent denial!" He cursed to no purpose.

"Why does it matter?" I asked him. He did not answer, but said: "You can bloody well believe what you like!"

"Tell you what—I'll look at what the poll tax does, rather than what you now say it is for. I'll base my beliefs on the evidence of the effects of the poll tax. Okay?" He grumbled for a minute or two, then appeared to accept that.'

Endquote. The Poll Tax Gerrymander gave the UK an unforecast-by-pollsters 4th Conservative victory and the undistinguished government of John Major. According to location 5061 of the Kindle version of Lord Robert Skidelsky's book "Britain since 1900 - A Success Story"

"...Margaret Thatcher's attempt to impose the Poll Tax in Scotland ahead of England - leading to 2.5 million summary warrants in a country [with a population] of 5 million..."

Scottish voters in 1987 totalled 2,967,808, so handing out 2.5 million warrants was to present half the population of the country and perhaps 83% of voters with a warrant.

One of the most thorough analysis of the 1992 Conservative victory was in the Independent on Sunday 29 May 1994, which said (among many other things)

"Poll tax de-registration. Our findings suggest that as many as 500,000 voters did not register because they wanted to avoid paying poll tax. The gain to the Conservatives' lead in overall votes was only 0.5 per cent, however. This is enough, in theory, to have cost Labour as many as seven extra seats and the Liberal Democrats three, but only if one makes some heroic assumptions about the distribution of the votes."

See http://www.independent.co.uk/news/uk/exclusive-how-did-labour-lose-in-92-the-most-authoritative-study-of-the-last-general-

election-is-published-tomorrow-here-its-authors-present-their-
conclusions-and-explode-the-myths-about-the-greatest-upset-
since-1945-1439286.html

That analysis, good in many ways, ignores the "fear factor." Many
registered voters who would have voted Labour but had not paid
their poll taxes were disinclined to vote because they believed the
police might catch them outside or at the ballot box. The police often
had a token presence around the voting locations, with the objective
of maintaining order, which fuelled these fears. Such fears were
irrational but nonetheless real. The British press invented the "shy
Conservative voter" to help explain Major's victory at the polls, but
the fearful non-poll-tax-payer and non-conservative voter who did
not vote is a major gerrymandered factor in that victory.

I am not sure how that study arrived at the number of 500,000 voters
not registering. It seems much too low, although a 1992 pamphlet by
Jeremy Smith and Iain McLean entitled "The UK poll tax and the
declining electoral roll: unintended consequences?" concluded that:

"In total the poll tax, it is estimated, can account for slightly more
than one-third of the estimated one million people shortfall between
the electoral register and the OPCS estimate of the qualified

population."

I think about 3m to 4m voters were originally disenfranchised, but
after a year to two, many of these voters were harried into paying the
poll tax and returned to the registers. While the 19m UK
householders and landlords saw their annual taxes reduced to a
fraction of their previous level, 24m tenants and other occupiers
received poll taxes for the first time. Many voters tried to de-register
but it was not an easy process - there was no system permitting de-
registration as such. Great changes were introduced by some voters
to avoid the poll tax and to incidentally remove themselves from the
Electoral Roll. The natural number of relocating voters rose
dramatically as renters moved to avoid the Poll Tax. Some moved
abroad on holiday and then returned to relocated multiple occupancy
locations. Most landlords and householders were unwilling to de-
register tenants or lodgers when the legally risked penalty was
£1,000. Shifting to the informal occupation of less well recorded
subtenancies increased, with one Poll Tax payment by the head

leaseholder and the many tenants occupying the property not being recorded for Poll Tax Purposes or on the electoral rolls.

The Poll Tax protesters numbered in the tens of millions. These protesters swamped the capability of the Police and Courts to handle them. As Wikipedia (see https://en.wikipedia.org/wiki/Community_Charge) reports

'The anti-poll tax organisations encouraged non-payers not to register, to clog up the courts by contesting Local Council attempts to gain liability orders, and ultimately to fail to attend court hearings for non-compliance. In November 1990, South Yorkshire police said they were planning to refuse to arrest poll tax defaulters even when instructed to by the courts because it would be "physically impossible for the police because of the large number of defaulters." '

The Poll Tax risked making the United Kingdom ungovernable. This seemed to be quite tolerable to Thatcher's Conservative Government if it produced the desired effect of a fourth Conservative victory at the polls.

Which it did.

The Poll Tax gerrymander produced the result that the Conservatives were elected with a popular vote of 11,334,328 while Labour received 9,344,328 votes, a Conservative votes majority of 2,532,543.

The total electorate was over 43.2 million and the turnout was 77.7%. The non-voters were about 9.6 million. If all the polls had been right, Labour might have had about 3 million to 4 million more votes. The question about how many Labour voters did not vote because of the Poll Tax is not a simple one, because the lost Labour voters were the disenfranchised plus the relocating voters who did not wish to re-register plus the "fear factor" non-paying voters who thought the polling day police might catch them. Kinnock might have become Prime Minister. Calculating the margin between the votes cast and the opinion polls - because all of the opinion polls prior to the 1992 election gave the Labour Party a slight lead - produces the quite credible result that the Poll Tax may have reduced the Labour vote by between 3 millions to 4 millions, and the Poll Tax therefore produced the surprise of the 4th Conservative victory.

3.3 4th May 2015 Article "Is Britain now Too Gerrymandered To Be A Genuine Democracy?" This article was published three days before the 7 May 2015 British General Election on at https://medium.com/@georgetaitedwards/is-britain-now-too-gerrymandered-to-be-a-genuine-democracy-fe2fcbd95d14

"1 The Gerrymandering Measures

During the last 27 years, Conservative and Coalition Governments have passed legislation aimed at reducing the voting rights of several groups of people whose votes are not likely to be supportive of the Conservative Party. These three main vexatious pieces of legislation are

The Poll Tax or Community Charge

The Bedroom Tax

The 2013 Individual Electoral Registration ("IER") and Administration Act

These pieces of legislation are gerrymandering devices masquerading as tax-raising (the Community Charge or Poll Tax) or cost-reducing (the Bedroom Tax) or improved voter registration (the 2013 Electoral Registration and Administration Act) when they are all actually gerrymandering legislation designed to chase some voters off the rolls. All of these measures have caused and are causing the denial of voting rights to presumed or mainly non-Conservative voters. These issues are considered in more detail in the following sections, which renames each Act according to its major effects.

2.1 The Poll Tax—"It's £400 a year for the right to vote" Poll taxes everywhere and always have been used to deny voting rights to a section of the electors in the population; it is in fact their only real function wherever they have been introduced. In the UK, the Electoral Roll was used to identify poll tax payers and many young and poorer voters decided to leave the Electoral Register rather than pay up to £400 a year for the right to vote. As Wikipedia comments (see http://en.wikipedia.org/wiki/Community_Charge) "There is also some evidence that the poll tax had a lasting effect of people not registering themselves on the electoral register to evade collection attempts. This may have had an effect on the results of the 1992 General Election, which ended in a fourth successive Conservative victory, despite most opinion polls pointing to a hung parliament or narrow Labour majority. "

In the USA , American Poll Taxes were used to disenfranchise poor people of Afro-American origin by setting the Poll Tax high enough to make voting rights unaffordable by black voters but easily affordable by whites. In the United Kingdom the Poll Charge was not specifically racist or misogynist but was aimed at deterring voter registration by poorer voters who were more likely to vote Labour. Poorer immigrants or poorly-paid women were of course disproportionately affected by the Poll Tax and it had the intended effect of removing many of these voters from the electoral roll but that was a side effect rather than its main targeted function. Many of the voters de-registered by the Poll Tax are still not re-registered in England but in Scotland a democratic uprising associated with the Scottish Independence Referendum has restored many previous non-voters to the Electoral Rolls.

Votes for women were won by decades of effective protest against unwilling governments. These hard won benefits of votes for women have been lost for many women because they are poor, due to this disgraceful Poll Tax gerrymandering.

2.2 The "Reduced Benefits" Bedroom Tax or "Move away or lose benefits" 'Ethic Cleansing of the Poor' Act In theory, the main justification for the bedroom tax is to save £500m a year by downsizing and right-sizing public housing to individual family needs. In practice, the loss of benefit for the poorest families and the official request that they should relocate up to hundreds of miles away to occupy cheaper and smaller public housing is equivalent to an ethnic cleansing of the poor by their relocation. In London 50,000 families have already been relocated, often far way from their previously occupied housing, despite Mayor Boris Johnson's statement that there would be no "ethic cleansing" of the poor in London. The relocation of more than 100,000 non-Conservative voters mainly out of London, away from the jobs, friends and social and family support structures they previously had, is a quite inhuman measure resulting in a loss of Labour votes in the capital. Relocating voters need to re-register on the Electoral Roll and while the "Bedroom Tax" appears to temporarily disenfranchise voters, it often produces a longer lasting denial of the right to vote. This Act affects/ disenfranchises about a million people.

2.3 The 2013 Individual Electoral Registration (IER) and Administration Act, or the 'Property Owner-Voter register, but Don't Register Tenants, or Spouses" Act This Act abolishes Household Electoral Registration (HER) and introduces individual voter registration (IER) and its stated aim is to improve the integrity of the voting register. Unfortunately the deliberately chosen method of implementation of this Act disenfranchises non-Conservative voters much more than it improves the integrity of the Electoral Roll. So while the intention is noble, the results are execrable.

The Act does three things: it requires that the landlord or householder should be registered, but it does not require the landlord or tenant to advise the Electoral Registration Authorities of other occupants of the premises, and it lowers to penalties for non-cooperation on registration of voters from £1,000 to a possible £80 or (since penalties are unlikely to be applied) to nil.

All Acts of Parliament (and all political leaders) should be judged by the results they produce and not by what it (or they) claim they intend to achieve. This Act operates as a kind of property qualification system because it prioritises landlord and householder registration while down-rating individual registration. This Act is disenfranchising students, tenants, spouses and younger voters by requiring them all to make individual applications rather than being included in a list prepared by the University, the landlord, or the householder. While appearing to improve the Electoral Roll integrity, this change requires individuals to know their National Insurance Number in order to register. Many students or younger people who are temporarily away from home do not know their National Insurance number so are disenfranchised. Many housewife-homemakers have not needed to know their NHS number for years.

As David Lindsay noted on 7 October 2011 (see http:// davidaslindsay.blogspot.co.uk/2011/10/great-gerrymander.html)

"Put simply, the Tories, aided and abetted by the Liberal Democrats, are rigging the rules of the electoral system to make it easier for themselves to win parliamentary majorities after 2015.

"How so? The switch from households to individuals, coupled with the lack of enforcement, will lead to a sharp decline in the number of registered voters (as happened in Northern Ireland when the switch was made there, in 2002). It is estimated that at present 3.5 million people eligible to vote (or one in ten) do not register to do so. According to Jenny Watson, chair of the Electoral Commission, under voluntary IER, the electoral register could go "from a 90 per cent completeness that we currently have to 60–65 per cent"—an astonishing ten million or more voters could just fall off the register.

"All of the empirical evidence suggests that those who tend not to register to vote are drawn disproportionately from the ranks of the young, the urban poor and ethnic minorities. These eligible voters, by complete coincidence, tend to support Labour."

David ends his article by saying"After the August 9 riots, David Cameron spoke of a "sick society". Yet his own reform of the electoral system will lead to a sick democracy, with fewer registered voters and lower turn-outs. It is the biggest political scandal you've never heard of."

3 Implications

3.1 Future British Governments should act to ensure the Electoral Rolls are up to date using information which they already have and then requesting local or individual verification of these revisions. The 2013 IER Act should be repealed. It beggars belief that the British Government pretend not to know who lives in Britain and where most of their population live. Government data has no difficulty in locating nearly everybody for tax purposes and the increasingly unified government data systems have complete registers of workers, drivers, and all benefit claimants, and their addresses. A more complete electoral register could be compiled by government from readily available data and checked by the local Electoral Registration Officers as required. This is, to a slight extent, how the new IER rolls are being established from the old ones, by listing in the new IER register the 35 million electors whose data can be fully cross-checked against only the existing DWP data. But that procedure disenfranchises over 11 million voters who are currently on the electoral roll and requires them all to make individual applications asap.

3.2 Britain needs a constitution to prevent the continuation of gerrymandering legislation Property cannot be used as the primary basis for voter registration in the USA, as it is being used in the 2013 IER Act. Government gerrymandering should be at least as illegal in the UK as it is in the USA. The 24th Amendment to the US constitution makes illegal any denial of the right to vote brought about by a Poll or other tax. See http://en.wikipedia.org/wiki/Twenty-fourth_Amendment_to_the_United_States_Constitution. Thatcher's Poll Tax would therefore have been illegal in the USA because it led to the disenfranchisement of non-payers.

3.3 There needs to be a better sense of morality in British political life. The actions of the Conservative Party in Government, using the power of the Coalition Government to pass Acts which disenfranchise these sections of the population who may be unlikely to vote Conservative, is a deep stain on the British political system and an affront to the democratic foundations of the British state.

3.4 It would help if less of the British Media were foreign-owned. The foreign-owned section of the British media appear to have no interest in investigating the damage done to the British democracy by voter-reducing Government gerrymandering.

4 Overarching Conclusions On 27 February 2015 the Electoral Commission reported that 920,000 voters—most of them young people and students—have disappeared during the 10 months to December 2014 from the electoral register. Cardiff and Oxford—cities with large student populations—have experienced a fall of over 10% in their electoral rolls. The third downward spiral in voter registration due to deliberate government action is now well underway. The abolition of the Annual Canvass removes a useful check on who lives where and ensures the Electoral Register does not get up to date between elections. See http://www.electoral-reform.org.uk/sites/default/files/MissingMillionsReport_FINAL(2).pdf

In my opinion the Conservative-led Coalition Government have gone too far—millions of disenfranchised votes too far -- in the 2013 IER legislation. The Conservatives are obviously no better at gerrymandering than they are at running the economy. A gerrymandered Conservative landslide in total opposition to all the polls is likely to produce an obviously illegally elected government.In my view the British Electoral Roll is now far too gerrymandered for Britain to be considered a a fully representative democracy. Two of the gerrymandering Acts listed above would have been illegal in the USA, where Poll Taxes and property-owner preference legislation are outlawed by the American constitution. The previous number of non-registered voters was 7.5 million, and now, thanks to the 2013 Individual Electoral Registration and Administration Act, there are 8.6 million unregistered potential voters. Furthermore, the new young voters—the "attainers" in electoral terms—has fallen by over 33% since February/March 2014, so another quarter of a million young "new voters" are likely to be disenfranchised. On 1 May 2013 there were 46,139,000 on the electoral register, now down by over a million. With 8.6 million missing voters in an Electoral Register of about 45 million that is a disfranchisement for more than one in six, or about 16% of the potentially voting population. The actual post-IER disenfranchisement is much more than that, probably in the range of 20 to 25 percent.

The net effect of the two most recent gerrymanders appears at first glance to be about a 4% decline in non-Conservative votes, but the real effect is certainly much larger than that. If the Conservatives win the 2015 election it will not be on the basis of their record, their policies or the issues, it will be because the Coalition Government have gerrymandered that politically scandalous result. The 7 May 2015 election of a widely hated and economically incompetent Conservative Government—not based upon any popular vote, but upon Coalition gerrymandering - looks likely.

In every sense of the words, that would be a rotten result.

Whether any government so elected—without any popular democratic mandate—can long survive, is an interesting question. The IER system if not repealed is likely to produce one-party Conservative Governments for at least a generation.

I venture to predict that this will be the last straw for the Scots, who will find a way to exit the corrupted Union. The rUK on its part will have to find a way of restoring the representative democracy which the Coalition has destroyed."

3.4 25th May 2015 "A Gerrymandered Election and A Flawed Mandate" - By Bryan Gould and George Tait Edwards

This article was originally published by Bryan Gould and George Tait Edwards on 25th May 2015 at: https://medium.com/ @georgetaitedwards/a-gerrymandered-election-and-a-flawed-mandate-6164fb125950 and on Saturday 30th May 2015 at http:// londonprogressivejournal.com/article/view/2205/a-gerrymandered-election-and-a-flawed-mandate

"To the great puzzlement and consternation of pundits and pollsters, the British general election produced what seems to have been a great democratic victory for the Conservative party. The result is, however, easily explained. It was based on the deliberate disenfranchisement of millions of people who were most unlikely to vote Conservative. It does not require great forensic skill to expose just how it was done.

The smoking gun was a seemingly innocuous piece of legislation called the Individual Electoral Registration and Administration Act, passed in 2013 with the support of the Electoral Commission. Its ostensible purpose was to reduce electoral fraud by ending the practice of allowing the head of household or the landlord of student digs or the warden of a student hostel and the like to enrol on the electoral register all those resident at a particular address, and to require instead that each elector should enrol individually. The supposedly unintended outcome was to drive millions of voters off the register.

We know it cannot have been unintended because the outcomes were widely foreseen. The Individual Electoral Registration system (IER) had already been given a trial run in Northern Ireland in 2002. A Wikipedia report—http://en.wikipedia.org/wiki/Electoral_Fraud_ %28Northern_Ireland%29_Act_2002 —records that "In August 2002 the last register of electors compiled [in Northern Ireland] under the old system contained nearly 1.2 million names, while the first register under the new system, published in December 2002, contained less than 1.1 million names, losing some 120,000 names for a net reduction of 10%."

It is therefore hard to accept that an outcome of this kind was an "unintended knock-on effect." And this is borne out by the many warnings issued by various commentators in the run–up to the 2015 general election.

The Electoral Reform Society had produced a very revealing "Missing Millions" Report in October 2011—see http://www.electoral-reform.org.uk/sites/default/files/MissingMillionsReport_FINAL(2).pdf. The individual comments of the authors are worth noting. Michael Summerville, for example, said "We have spent years building up the register. We're concerned that all that work will be undone. We could be looking at a 20–30,000 drop from a register of 165,000."

Lewis Baston, Senior Research Fellow, Democratic Audit, voiced concern that parliamentary boundaries will be [re]drawn on the new electoral register, describing it as "utterly frightening". Lewis outlined further concerns that "if after 2015 the register is purged of the last household canvass this will make the next boundary review taking place in 2016–2018 incomplete."

Chris Ruane MP (Vale of Clwyd) was forthright in his views: "The people who are going to be left off are poor, black and ethnic, and living in privately rented and social housing. We're going to return to electoral registration rates like Alabama in the 1950s" and **Simon Wooley, from the Operation Black Vote,** remarked "There won't be the resources or the political will to deal with a massive democratic deficit"

Peter Facey, from Unlock Democracy, noted "the ongoing review of parliamentary boundaries" and that "the connection is problematic given the close proximity in terms of timings." He referred to the view "the timing of IER taken together with the boundary review could give rise to the perception that the reforms were motivated by partisan interests. As a result, some participants supported the view that either the introduction of IER or boundary review should be delayed."

And the Electoral Reform Society itself concluded "The Electoral Reform Society shares the views of electoral registration officers and others that existing plans have failed to sufficiently guard against a drop in the completeness of the register, and that in particular, traditionally disadvantaged groups within society risk further exclusion from the political process."

The media had begun to take notice in 2014. On 3 July 2014, **the BBC** reported for example that a "Publicity campaign begins to highlight voting changes" at http://www.bbc.co.uk/news/uk-politics-28132233 and raised a belated curtain on the Coalition Government's proposal to amend voter registration procedures.

The Huffington Post on 2 December 2014, at http://www.huffingtonpost.co.uk/sadiq-khan/2015-election-voter-registration_b_6255392.html) had published an article by Sadiq Khan in which he commented that "Alas, people not on the register aren't isolated cases. The Electoral Commission estimate that 7.5 million people who are eligible to vote are unregistered—that's ten cities the size of Sheffield. And, as a result of the move to IER, the Electoral Commission themselves have estimated that a further 5.5 million people are at risk of dropping off the register.

And it's private renters, the BAME [Black and Middle East] community, young people and students who are most vulnerable to falling off the register. Just this week data showed how important student voters could be in a number of crucial battleground seats, making this issue doubly important to the outcome of the next election.So many people missing off the register would mean decisions on the future of the country are decided by a smaller and smaller group of people, with political parties gearing their policies towards those they know vote. It is self-reinforcing, and risks corroding our democracy from the inside out."

The Huffington Post returned to the charge on 2 March 2015, reporting that a million voters had fallen off the electoral roll within the last year—see http://www.huffingtonpost.co.uk/2015/02/02/one-million-voters-have-fallen-off-britains-electoral-register_n_6600740.html and that "Most affected by the drop off are students, with government reform of the individual electoral registration resulting in a steep decline in voter registration in university towns. The reform was designed to prevent electoral fraud, but the unintended knock-on effect has been to disenfranchise a million potential voters."

The Huffington Post report explained further: "Previously, universities were able to register students in bulk, usually by their halls of residence. However, the government no longer allows this. Young adults, particularly those living in private rented accommodation, have also been squeezed, as have newer immigrant communities. Cities adversely affected—losing thousands of voters each—include Leeds, Brighton, Birmingham, Cardiff, Lancaster,

Newcastle and the outer fringes of London including Dagenham. Remarkably, the reforms have left some universities, such as East Sussex, with a near-90% drop in [student] voters, plunging from 3,500 registered students in 2014 to just 377 this year. Incredibly, Scotforth ward in Lancaster has only 22 of it[s] 7,000 students registered to vote, a shortfall that will have profound implications at the general election."

As the date of the general election approached, **Ed Miliband became alarmed**. He said "This is a direct consequence of the government's decision to ignore warnings that rushing through new individual registration reforms would damage democracy. We will not allow this scandal to happen and no right-thinking person should either." But it was too late. Neither Ed Miliband nor any "right-thinking person" could prevent this scandal from happening.

The Guardian had picked up the theme on 24 February 2014—see http://www.theguardian.com/uk-news/2015/feb/24/million-voters-missing-roll-electoral-commission-students-block-individual-registration where Patrick Wintour and Matthew Taylor reported a drop in the electoral roll numbers by 920,000 "in the 10 months to December 2014, with some areas—including Cardiff and Oxford which both have large student populations—seeing falls of more than 10%."

Paul Wheeler, the Founder of the Political Skills Forum, also reported on Thursday 5 February under the headline "Britain's missing voters: why individual registration has been a disaster" (see http://www.theguardian.com/public-leaders-network/2015/feb/05/missing-voters-individual-electoral-registration-disaster) that "[A further] Seven million people risk being removed from the voting register if they do not provide evidence of where they live by December 2015."

And, while the Cabinet Office insisted that "the switch to individual voter registration will not affect the general election since anyone on the old household register in December 2013 will be entitled to vote in 2015", that turned out not to be the case. As Mr Wheeler reports, "The burden has been put on cash-strapped local councils to contact 46 million voters instead of 20 million households. Some have been able to, but many simply don't have the money or IT skills.

We have made a simple process of registration much more complex. For instance, a newly-married woman who chooses to change her name is now required to provide two forms of identification before being accepted back on to the register. But the group most affected is students. Previously, universities, like other institutional landlords, could provide a single list of eligible voters to the local authority. Now every student has to register individually. That is not necessarily a priority during freshers' week. The result is levels of registration plummeting from 100% to less than 10% in most university residences."

In **The Guardian of 21 February 2014, Rowenna Davis** had asked "What is the real motive behind individual voter registration?" see http://www.theguardian.com/commentisfree/2014/feb/21/individual-voter-registration-conservative-party. She observed that the major justification for IER was said to be to prevent fraud, but that, since there is no evidence of widespread fraud, the remedy is worse than the alleged problem. She commented "The government says that individual voter registration is needed to prevent fraud, and I expect it would reject Labour's proposed solutions on the same grounds. The problem is that there is no evidence to support its position. According to the Electoral Commission, there have been less than 10 proven cases of electoral registration fraud in the past four years, and it's not clear how this new system—which allows you to register online without a paper trail or signature to check—can solve this problem. Even if by some weird twist the government proposals did reduce fraud, the cost in terms of potentially thousands of people dropping off the register and being turned away at the polls doesn't seem worth it. Why should the wrongs of a few mean that the many are punished?"

Her conclusion was that "Sadly, I fear it is in the Conservative party's interest to suppress the number of citizens who are able to vote. This is a party that opposed universal suffrage and caused a massive decline in the number of people on the electoral roll through Margaret Thatcher's plans for a poll tax, which resulted in many people dropping off the list for fear of having to pay. The party knows that the groups vulnerable to the change—renters, BME groups, young people—are unlikely to vote for it. The groups left voting will be the relatively powerful in society, and so our politics will become more likely to serve them and their interests, cutting the less fortunate out of the conversation."

It cannot be credible that these expressions of concern did not constitute an adequate warning that the franchise would be prejudicially affected as so many voters dropped off the register. Yet the Government was not to be deterred. Indeed, the British system exhibited several features that made the problems worse.

Other jurisdictions had managed to introduce an individual electoral registration system without producing such disastrous consequences. The Australians, for example, transferred to an IER system without disenfranchising millions of their voters. (See http://www.aec.gov.au/About_AEC/research/direct.htm [Also see Section 3.5 below.] The Australian achievement of a functioning representative democracy with an enviably complete voters roll is a gold standard for others to emulate. The chosen method of implementation of the Coalition Government's IER Act maximised the loss of voters by specifying that every change of address and every change of name (such as on marriage) would require a new individual registration on each occasion, accompanied by proofs of identification. The disincentive effect was thereby maximised.

The Coalition Government did its best to conceal the scale of what was happening. Nearly all UK Electoral Statistics released by the Coalition Government are based upon comparisons with a previous year or with an earlier month in the year. These are misleading because they take no account of the movement between 2015 and earlier dates over a longer period.

The Office for National Statistics, for example, says that "The total number of UK parliamentary electors in 2013 was 46,139,900, a fall of 0.5% from 2012." and that "The number of parliamentary electors has declined in all regions of England between 2012 and 2013. The largest decrease (1.7%) was in the West Midlands." See http://www.ons.gov.uk/ons/rel/pop-estimate/electoral-statistics-for-uk/2013/stb---2013-electoral-statistics.html

But if we compare that with the December 2014 registers at http://www.electoralcommission.org.uk/__data/assets/pdf_file/0008/182375/Analysis-of-the-December-2014-electoral-registers-in-England-and-Wales.pdf we can see that the major losers of electoral votes are the university cities and those with relocating populations. Section 2 of that Report states "The "Live Run" to test out the number of voters in the IER system, taking place in July 2014, involved the matching of existing entries on the electoral registers against the Department for Work and Pensions (DWP) database as well as locally held data in order to identify which records could be automatically transferred to the IER registers. This process known as the 'Confirmation Live Run' (CLR), took place in June and July 2014 in England and Wales" and "Entries for electors that could be positively matched were confirmed and transferred directly to the new IER register. Those individuals not matched were written to by their ERO and asked to re-register by providing additional information (National Insurance number (NIN) and date of birth). Based on the CLR data matching (figure 1 below): 87% of entries on the June registers in England and Wales—totalling 36.9 million register entries—were positively matched and directly transferred to the new IER register. 13% of entries—totalling approximately 5.5 million—could not be matched."

So, while the total numbers on the English and Wales Electoral Roll could have been 42.4 million, only 36.9 million were directly transferred and 5.5 million were not registered. While these missing voters were allegedly being positively pursued using the measures listed in Section 4 of the Report, it is clear that cash-strapped local authorities might not have had either the money or the resources to find and register these missing voters.

Furthermore, there were, according to the Electoral Commission, 7.5 million missing voters not included even in the highest estimates of the Electoral Roll, so **the total Electoral Roll could and should be about (46 million + 7.5 million) or 53.5 million while those not registered to vote are (7.5 plus 5.5) million or 13 million, or about 24% missing voters.**

The pollsters seem not to have registered any of this information which provided, after all, a strong indication that a Conservative victory was likely. The British Polling Council (BPC) has announced that it proposes to conduct an enquiry into how the pollsters got it so wrong. See http://www.huffingtonpost.co.uk/2015/05/08/general-election-polls-enquiry_n_7244892.html . This investigation, if it has any quality, is bound to conclude that the Coalition government's 2013 IER legislation was responsible for the failure to predict the election outcome. It will probably put "unintentionally" before the word "responsible". We'll see.

In the meantime, we can be certain that at least a substantial part of the answer to the mystery of the unexpected Tory majority has been laid bare. **It is clear that many potential voters, particularly students and other young people, members of minority communities, those who move addresses frequently including many tenants, the poor and less well-educated, failed to enrol and therefore dropped off the electoral roll. It was these voters who made up the great majority of the five plus million voters who disappeared between 2010 and 2015. It is not fanciful to assume that many of these disenfranchised voters would have voted anything but Tory.** The impact of this kind of movement in marginal constituencies can easily be evaluated. A restricted franchise has always been seen as an advantage to the parties of the right—it was one of the objectives of the poll tax, after all—and it may well have operated as a very effective secret weapon.So, in the search for an explanation for the unexpected election result, we do not have far to look.

In addition to the perennial tendency towards a lower turnout by disadvantaged and younger voters, and the huge disparity in financial resources and media support enjoyed by right-wing parties, we can now identify a further built-in and deliberately engineered gerrymandering of the election process. We should never underestimate the ruthlessness with which the right pursues its goals. It can truly be said that they have at last discovered a mechanism for making democracy work for them."

****

On the basis of my calculations, on 6th May 2015 (the day before the election) I did a terrible and shameful thing. I went with my family to the nearest brach of Ladbroke's and we bet £350 on the Conservatives winning an overall majority in the 7th May 2015 election, and we got odds of 7 to 1 against that happening.

The following day we collected £2,800.

3.5 A Comparison of the Australian Implementation of Individual Electoral Registration with the Cameron-led Coalition Government's implementation of the 2013 IER Act

The Australians transferred to an Individual Electoral System by using a Continuous Roll Update (CRU) of their electoral rolls. That system involved using all the additional information available to the Australian government to maximise voter registration. Most of the following quotes in this section are from http://www.aec.gov.au/ about_aec/research/direct.htm, which reports:

"Prior to 1999 the Australian Electoral Commission (AEC) updated the roll using habitation reviews, which involved door-knocking of addresses across Australia's states and territories to confirm enrolments (AEC 2005). Habitation reviews were time consuming (taking up to six months to complete) and expensive around $16 million in 1999 dollars), and occurred only once every two years. Changing residential patterns and increasing population mobility made periodic habitation reviews a less effective roll maintenance strategy (AEC 1999)."

The previous Australian system therefore resembled the UK's Household Electoral Review. That source continues [italics introduced by me]:

"In 1999 the AEC in conjunction with its joint roll partners, the state and territory electoral commissions, introduced a new process for updating the roll called Continuous Roll Update (CRU). CRU matches data obtained *from various state and commonwealth government agencies* against the roll to identify individuals who have moved or who might not be correctly enrolled. The AEC also has an address register of habitable addresses and can identify when there are no (or too many) electors enrolled at an address. When the data matching process identifies potential enrolment variations the individual is sent a letter and enrolment form asking them to confirm their new details (ECA 2005). The enrolment is not updated until the individual returns a signed enrolment form to the AEC or an objection action is commenced by the AEC (see below).

The first iteration of CRU in 1999 involved the receipt of 600 000 change of address notifications from Australia Post. The response rate to the initial mail out was 32.3 per cent (ECA 1999). A report by the Australian National Audit Office in 2001 into the integrity of the electoral roll found that CRU was an effective means of managing the roll and would provide a roll that was "highly accurate, complete and valid" (ANAO 2002, 13). Two years into the operation of CRU, ANAO found that while the process was beneficial, the data used for CRU was not consistent across states and territories."

So the Australians used multiple data sources to ensure their voter registration was as complete as it could be. The Cameron-led Coalition Government decided to use one data source - the DWP records - to verify voter electoral records.The first attempt to match these records was known as the Confirmation Live Run (CLR) and was held in England and Wales in June and July 2014. That CLR resulted in 13% of previous voters being not matched. Why was the DWP system used alone? Why were other UK Government databases not used to ensure a more complete voter registration in the UK? Was there no objective in the introduction of IER in the UK except for the partisan aim of disenfranchising mainly non-Conservative voters? As Sadiq Khan commented in the Huffington Post in an article entitled "We Must Throw Our Weight Behind Voter Registration, Or Face a Crisis of Confidence in Our Democracy" (see http:// www.huffingtonpost.co.uk/sadiq-khan/2015-election-voter-registration_b_6255392.html):

"Government departments have enormous amounts of data about us at their disposal. Surely it is possible to have a system in place where people are automatically placed on the register on the basis of being on council tax lists, housing benefit databases or having applied for a passport or driving licence?"

But that would improve voter registration which was not the aim of Cameron-led Coalition Government policy.

As the AEC report reports, the Australians continually improved their system for voter registration:

"In 2004–05 4.1 million change of address and new potential elector records were received, primarily from Australia Post, Centrelink and motor vehicle licensing authorities. The resulting 2.4 million letters from the AEC resulted in 1.4 million responses, a response rate of 55 per cent (ECA 2005). Following the recommendations of the 2002 ANAO report the AEC also undertook Sample Audit Fieldwork

(SAF). The SAF exercise aimed to test the accuracy and completeness of the roll by door-knocking in 225 randomly selected Census Collection Districts (CCDs). The 2005 SAF found enrolment participation at 98.4 per cent, enrolment completeness at 96.3 per cent, and enrolment accuracy at 91.1 per cent (AEC 2005). The positive results from the SAF appeared to validate the effectiveness of CRU, and SAF exercises undertaken in 2006, 2007 and 2009 produced comparable results (AEC 2011a)."

As remarked above, other available UK Government databases were not used to improve the coverage of the UK IER electoral rolls. The Australian participation, completeness and accuracy levels are not approached by the UK IER system. Furthermore, if the elector consents the Australian electoral rolls can be updated without voter involvement:

"The idea of using the same information as the CRU to enrol an individual or update their details without requiring the individual to take any action is not a new one."

And

"On 23 June 2012 the Electoral and Referendum Amendment (Protecting Elector Participation) Bill 2012 and the Electoral and Referendum Amendment (Maintaining Address) Bill 2011 were passed by the Senate. These bills respectively allow the AEC to directly enrol and directly update eligible electors."

What "directly enrol" and "directly update" (abbreviated as DE/U) means are specified as

"This report discusses systems by which electoral management bodies (EMBs) can use administrative data from other agencies to enrol an individual or update the details of an already enrolled elector without the intervention of that individual."

And

"In practice, the electoral management body receives data from other agencies, including vehicle registration and licencing authorities and other bodies such as utilities and higher education authorities. These data are subjected to predefined business rules to determine their validity, with suitably trustworthy and verified data then prompting processes to add eligible individuals to the roll, or change the enrolment information of those already on the roll, without the intervention of the individual. The individual is then notified of their enrolment or enrolment change, and given the opportunity to dispute that change. If no objection is received, the roll is updated with the new information by the commission and the elector is notified to that effect."

The British IER system uses no other source except for an individual response to add to IER voter records. Why doesn't it? The only possible answer is that the default setting of the 2013 IER Act is voter de-registration which can be "blamed" on the voter but is actually a consequence of Government policy.

And the Australians also have an "Election Day Enrolment (EDE)" system. "Another electoral reform which has in practice been tightly coupled with DE/U is the ability to enrol, or change an existing enrolment, on election day at the polling place. Again, the systems in place currently in NSW and Victoria are different in practice, but share the same putative objective. For convenience, this general approach will be referred to as "election day enrolment" (EDE)."

And

"In Victoria and NSW, election day enrolment (EDE) is seen as an essential part of the direct enrolment and update strategy. Election day enrolment provides an opportunity for individuals who have been directly enrolled or updated to update incorrect details. It also enables individuals who are not affected by direct enrolment and update who attend at a voting centre on election day to enrol and vote. This affects the concept of a "close of rolls" date. The close of rolls is still an essential part of Victorian electoral administration and communications. The VEC emphasizes the need to enrol or update enrolment by the close of rolls, and regards election day enrolment as a savings provision to cater for people who for whatever reason have failed to either enrol or update their enrolment details in time."

The use of election day enrolment was urged on the UK Coalition Government during the implementation of IER, but the Government refused to consider it.

At every point, the Cameron-led Coalition Government chose the implementation option of the 2013 IER act which minimised voter participation, while the AEC defaulted the other way to maximise voter participation.

The conclusion about the Cameron-led implementation of the 2013 IER act can only be that the entire system was designed to gerrymander the electoral rolls by minimising voter registration to produce a partisan advantage in the Polling Booth.

The Electoral Commission's *Analysis of the December 2014 electoral registers in England and Wales: The implementation of Individual Electoral Registration: progress report* produced in February 2015, a mere three months before the election. (See the full copy of that report at http://www.electoralcommission.org.uk/__data/assets/pdf_file/0008/182375/Analysis-of-the-December-2014-electoral-registers-in-England-and-Wales.pdf). The Electoral Commission Paper records all the deficiencies, limitations and the objections made to the implementation of the 2013 IER Act and makes recommendations aimed at achieving a more complete registration of voters while the House of Commons Briefing paper records what happened and what is happening and lists Government decisions. The EC Report notes:

"The December registers contained approximately 920,000 fewer entries than the registers published in February/March 2014 following the 2013 canvass, which indicates a decrease of approximately 2%.

The decrease in the electorate is likely to be the result of the lack of comprehensive household canvass activity in 2014. Household Enquiry Forms (HEFs) – which are designed to identify who is living at a property and eligible to register so that the ERO can invite them to register to vote – were only required to be sent to properties where no electors were registered, or where the ERO believed there may still be other people living at the address who were not registered.

This means that home-movers have not been captured as effectively as they would have been during a typical annual canvass where all households would receive a form."

The Confirmation Live Run (CLR) held on June and July 2014 successfully matched 79% of voters against DWP data and a further 7% of voters were matched by EROs against local data. However 13% (5.5 million) of the previous electorate were not matched. This compares with the Northern Ireland 2003 experience of IER introduction when 10.5% of the previous electorate were lost as voters. The source of Figure 1 below is page 17 of the Analysis of the December 2014 electoral registers in England and Wales:

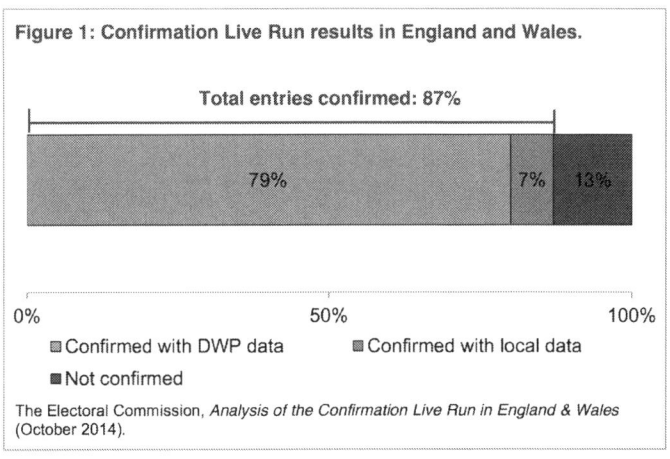

Figure 1: Confirmation Live Run results in England and Wales.

Total entries confirmed: 87%

79%   7%   13%

0%   50%   100%

■ Confirmed with DWP data   ■ Confirmed with local data
■ Not confirmed

The Electoral Commission, *Analysis of the Confirmation Live Run in England & Wales* (October 2014).

Further work was done to reduce the overall loss of voters as set out in chapter 4 in the report and the report was able to say:

"While the total number of electoral register entries in England and Wales decreased by 2% against the February/March 2014 figures, the variation at local level ranges from -12% to +7%. It is likely that there is even greater variation by electoral ward although we do not have detailed data at this level."

Digging down into the report it is clear that much more significant than the 2% decrease in voters, is the distribution of that decrease. Areas with the largest percentage decreases are mainly university towns or locations with large numbers of re-locating voters - Ceredigion with -12%, Cardiff -11%, Oxford -11%, Southampton -10%, Newcastle upon Tyne -9%, Haringey -9%, Charnwood -9%, Westminster -8%, Blackpool -8%, Reading -8%.

The outcome of the 2015 General Election would certainly been affected in each of these areas by these lost voters who were mainly students, council house tenants and re-locating persons who were unlikely to vote Conservative.

In some areas mainly in Southern England the number of voters went up in areas which were usually Conservative. The extra votes in Conservative areas were much less significant than the loss of Labour votes largely in Northern England and the Midlands. On a regional basis the North-West and North-East regions of England experienced voter losses of above 3%.

These lost voters at local level were much more significant than the frequently quoted overall reduction in voters of 2% or 920,000, often said to be mainly students.

3.6 11th June 2015 "What if David Cameron is a Gerrymandering PM?"*This article was originally published on June 11th 2015 at* https://medium.com/@georgetaitedwards

"On 1 June, Frankie Boyle the Scottish comedian used the Comment is Free section of the Guardian to ask the question "What if David Cameron is an Evil Genius?"—See

http://www.theguardian.com/commentisfree/2015/jun/01/david-cameron-moriarty-downing-street-radical-thatcher

"Prime Minister David Cameron is certainly evil but lacks the required judgement and has insufficient ability to cover his tracks. The Conservative win in the 7 May General Election had nothing to do with his intelligence or his lack of it. That win was due to the Coalition Government taking political control of the Electoral Rolls via the 2013 Individual Electoral Registration and Administration Act, and using the power of parliament to deliberately remove millions of non-Conservative voters from these rolls. See the article fully quoted in section 3.4 above.

The Individual Electoral Registration and Administration Act 2013 is probably the most democracy-damaging Act ever passed in any Western nation. The Coalition Government could not easily pass a legal act forbidding non-conservative voters the vote—that would make its intentions far too clear—so under Cameron's leadership it did what was apparently considered as the "next best" thing—slicing away at the democratic foundations of the British state by using the 2013 IER to disenfranchise mainly non-Conservative voters—the poor, students, the black and middle east (BME) communities, women (who have borne the brunt of the financial cuts so far), relocating voters, tenants, and those dependent on benefits. That 2013 IER Act gives the British Government complete control over the electoral rolls—the power to abandon the annual the Household Electoral review (HER) in any year; the power to decide whether to destroy previous, more widely based, HERs which have a more complete register of parliamentary electors; the power to create new versions of the electoral roll using the review powers of the Government; the power to decide, on a partisan basis, which "updated" or version of the electoral roll will be used in any General

Election; and the power to control Britain's future through the continued gerrymandering of the Electoral Roll without any constraint or oversight of Government activities in this area.

During the 2015 General Election Cameron stated that he would do anything to remain Prime Minister. He clearly has. The UK Electoral Rolls are meant to be an objective register of all these people over 18 who have the right to vote in a British General Election. The Government of the day is not meant to pass any Act restricting the right to vote by disenfranchising millions of its people for partisan political advantage. Yet that is exactly what the Coalition Government has done.

The Coalition Deputy Prime Minister, David Clegg, who agreed to the Coalition Government trebling of student fees in English Higher Education from £3,000 a year to £9,000 a year, voted for the 2013 IER which disenfranchised 920,000 students studying in England. There was a 2001 trial run of the IER Act in Northern Ireland (see http://en.wikipedia.org/wiki/Electoral_Fraud_%28Northern_Ireland %29_Act_2002) which records that "In August 2002 the last register of electors compiled [in Northern Ireland] under the old system contained nearly 1.2 million names, while the first register under the new system, published in December 2002, contained less than 1.1 million names, losing some 120,000 names for a net reduction of 10%." Many of these disenfranchised were students, and it is reasonable to assume Clegg knew all about that. Not content with trebling student fees when he had promised he wouldn't, Clegg voted for disenfranchising 920,000 students who were no longer likely to vote Liberal Democrat or Conservative.

The history of Conservative gerrymandering during the last 30 years is instructive. Thatcher's Community Charge, commonly known as the Poll Tax, removed millions of voters from the electoral rolls and provided the first pollsters-defying and fourth successive Conservative victory through gerrymandering. (See https://medium.com/@georgetaitedwards/thatcher-s-poll-tax-gerrymander-112ffe2e918e). Poll taxes have never been about raising government funds. Any mention of the Community Charge as a Poll Tax, which is what it was, immediately raises an objection from Conservatives that the tax should be referred to as a Community

Charge because Poll Taxes everywhere and always have been used to deny poorer and disadvantaged sections of the electorate the vote.

The Poll Tax initially reduced the Electoral Rolls by over 4m voters, the "bedroom tax" is still on its way to reduce the rolls by about 1.5 million voters, and the 2013 IER Act further reduced the Electoral Rolls by 5.5 million voters, with a further 7m voters are reported as likely to drop off the register by December 2015 if they do not provide identifying data.

It is very, very unwise for Cameron and the Conservative Government to imagine that gerrymandering on this epic scale could possibly not be noticed and would be acceptable to the British people. The hated Poll Tax provided a fourth unlikely Conservative victory and the weak and undistinguished John Major Government. The 2013 IER Act, if a greater measure of democracy is not restored in the United Kingdom, could result in stunning Conservative victories perhaps forever. Conservative Governments could choose, as the Coalition Government has chosen, a limited subset of voters which were mainly conservative and could continue to deny the proper operation of the democratic process in the United Kingdom for much of the 21st century. Only a very unwise person could imagine that process could continue for decades.

It would not be so bad if the Cameron Government had any positive programme for higher growth in the United Kingdom or any understanding of economic growth. But they do not. (For a much better economic understanding , see https://medium.com/@georgetaitedwards/shimomuran-economics-is-the-most-significant-advance-ever-made-in-economic-understanding-and-the-e540e58bf270). Osborne thinks economics is only about the Government making economies. The major programme of the 2015 Conservative Government is the victimisation of the groups they have disenfranchised. Access to higher education in the UK now costs £9,000 a year and higher education in England is becoming as it was in previous centuries—a privilege-creating enclave for the relatively rich. 75% of the people affected by the "Bedroom Tax" are disabled and that tax is a deliberate attack on the living standards of disabled people who generally do not vote Conservative. The reduction of benefits to poorer people who are often members of the Black and Middle East Communities is a racialist measure whatever its political or cost-saving justification. The denial of voting rights to women who are occupying poorly paid jobs is an appalling reversal of women's hard-won right to vote. Cameron could have better judgement, but he hasn't. His major programme is an attack on the living standards of the non-Conservative voters.

Davis Cameron is no "Evil Genius." He is unfortunately a gerrymandering politician, along with his cronies. He is a kind of British Nixon, a lack of brightness might not be his problem, his problem is a lack of sound judgement in this and many other issues. The House of Commons tried to stop the progress of the Individual Registration and Administration Bill 2013 and their concerns were noted on an Early Day Motion proposed by Valerie Vaz and duly recorded at http://www.parliament.uk/edm/2010-12/2208. That motion reads:

"That this House notes with concern the potential implications for democracy of the Government's proposals to introduce individual electoral registration before the 2015 elections; further notes that the Government has decided there will be no electoral canvass in 2014; is concerned by the Electoral Commission's view that the level of completeness of the electoral register could fall from approximately 90 per cent. to around 65 per cent. as a result of the complexity of the changes and the Government's opt out proposal, whereby it would be no longer compulsory to co-operate with electoral registration officers; is further concerned that registration under these changes is likely to be lower in inner-city areas and among the young; further notes that this may have important implications for the population of Walsall South; recognises that the electoral register is of vital importance not only for enabling people to vote but also for determining future representation and electoral boundaries; and calls on the Government to undertake a full canvass in 2014 in order to explain any changes and maintain completeness of the register, to promote the importance of electoral registration as an important civic duty, and to ensure legitimate democratic representation."

The Coalition Government charged on, to gerrymander the electoral rolls and produce a partisan advantage through that Act. There was no electoral canvass in 2014. The level of completeness of the electoral rolls has fallen substantially, partly because there is no longer any compulsion to provide the required information to the

Electoral Registration Officers. And the Coalition Government created a reduced version of the Electoral Rolls so that they could subvert democracy and bring into play that "Electoral Roll" which maximised their partisan advantage, while claiming it was all being done to avoid abuses in electoral registration.

The first attempt to implement the IER 2013 Act was "Confirmation Live Run" (CLR) conducted in July 2014 where

"Entries for electors that could be positively matched were confirmed and transferred directly to the new IER register. Those individuals not matched were written to by their ERO and asked to re-register by providing additional information (National Insurance number (NINO) and date of birth). Based on the CLR data matching (figure 1 below): 87% of entries on the June registers in England and Wales— totalling 36.9 million register entries—were positively matched and directly transferred to the new IER register. 13% of entries— totalling approximately 5.5 million—could not be matched."

So an overview of the UK "Electoral rolls" position would read that the number of total potential voters over 18 and entitled to vote could be about 46.2 million plus 7.5 missing voters, or 53.7 million potential total voters. The development of the three parliamentary electoral roll lists which could have been used for the GE 2015 were:

1 Electoral Roll List 1 (ELR1) : ONS 2013 voters on the Electoral Roll: 46.2 million voters. This was the list the Cabinet promised would be used, but it wasn't, because it would have produced a Labour-SNP government.

2 Electoral Roll List 2 (ERL2) : CLR June/July 2014 IER-reduced English Voters: 36.9 million. This was the first IER "Confirmation Live Run" list which matched voters against Department of Work and Pensions records and which disenfranchised millions (compared to the ONS list) of English-based largely non-conservative voters by removing them from the rolls.

3 Electoral List 3: Section 5.6 of the Parliamentary Standard Note SN/PC/06764 on Individual Electoral Registration updated on 3 February 2015, prepared by Isobel White of the Parliament and Constitution Centre, states that:

"The final match rate, after matching with DWP and local data, across Great Britain was 87%. These figures mean that overall approximately 40.5 million electors were matched."And 5.7 million potential voters were disenfranchised, compared with the ONS 2013 list. This was the updated "best available" electoral roll resulting from the implementation if the 2013 IER Act.

Now suppose you were a Prime Minister of the United Kingdom who lacked judgement and your government had taken over the control of the electoral rolls and that takeover was so complete that you thought nobody could see what you were doing. And suppose you would, as you had announced to the world, "Do anything to remain Prime Minister." Might you be tempted to use the latest 2013 IER Act list which more or less guaranteed the election of a Conservative Government? And might the Cabinet Office be persuaded to say, as they promised would occur, that the December 2013 ONS list was used in the 7 May 2015 General Election when it wasn't?"

The House of Commons Library Briefing Paper Number 6764, dated 21 July 2015 entitled *Individual Electoral Registration* and authored by Isobel White, commented on page 20 upon the Government decision to end the transition to IER in December 2015, pointing out the views of the Electoral Commission:

"The data we have collected from EROs tells us that if the transition ended now, the registers would decrease in size by 1.9 million entries, with some registers decreasing significantly more than others. While there is still work to be done between now and December 2015 which we expect will reduce this number, it does provide an indication of the maximum potential impact of ending the transition this year."

One of the most frequent comments made, when people are advised about Cameron's gerrymandering of the Parliamentary Electoral Rolls, is that The Right Honourable David Cameron would not stoop so low as to destroy much of the foundation of British democracy in order to deliver the partisan objective of a Conservative majority in the House of Commons.

But he did. He has. He's still doing it. He needs to be stopped and prevented from ever doing that again using the usual democratic process, because he plans much worse to follow, as sections 3.8 and 4.1 following illustrate.

3.7 Britain's Inadequate Media

I think the biggest story in the United Kingdom is the Conservative gerrymandering of the Parliamentary Electoral Rolls so as to produce the Conservative Victory in the 7 May 2015 General Election. Yet there is no informed discussion of that event in any of the national or international media after the date of the 7 May 2015 election although there were several beacon articles before then. That seems astonishing.

Of course, I have not read every newspaper or watched every TV programme so I cannot be sure that there has been no post-election newspaper or TV coverage of this issue. But there has been no major coverage of the kind that everyone would notice and this would be surprising if the British Press were as free and as objective as it claims.

Prior to the election there were reports of the intended gerrymandering, or the forecast effects of the 2013 IER Act, in the following articles, which have been referenced elsewhere in this book, and which are quoted here to contrast pre-election and post-election comments:

On 11th October 2011, as reported in Section 3.3 p2, David Lindsay forecast the likely affect of the 2013 IER Act as a gerrymandering device (see http://davidaslindsay.blogspot.co.uk/2011/10/great-gerrymander.html).

On 3rd July 2014 the BBC reported that a *Publicity campaign begins to highlight voting changes (see* http://www.bbc.co.uk/news/uk-politics-28132233)

On 2nd December 2014 the Huffington Post published an article called *We Must Throw Our Weight Behind Voter Registration, Or Face a Crisis of Confidence in Our Democracy* written by Sadiq Khan, the Labour MP for Tooting, and standing to be Labour's Mayoral candidate for London in 2016 (see http://www.huffingtonpost.co.uk/sadiq-khan/2015-election-voter-registration_b_6255392.html) There was no post-election follow-up to this article.

Paul Vale's report on 3rd February 2015 in the Huffington Post about *One Million Voters Have Fallen Off Britain's Electoral Register*

written by Paul Vale (see http://www.huffingtonpost.co.uk/
2015/02/02/one-million-voters-have-fallen-off-britains-electoral-
register_n_6600740.html) should perhaps have been followed up. It
wasn't.

There was also no post-election follow-up in the Guardian to
Rowenna Davis' 21 February 2014 excellent article where she asked
"What is the real motive behind individual voter registration?" (see
http://www.theguardian.com/commentisfree/2014/feb/21/individual-
voter-registration-conservative-party). Again, why not?

Patrick Wintour and Matthew Taylor in the Guardian 24th February
2014 reported a drop in the electoral roll numbers by 920,000 "in the
10 months to December 2014, with some areas—including Cardiff
and Oxford which both have large student populations—seeing falls
of more than 10%."(see http://www.theguardian.com/uk-news/2015/
feb/24/million-voters-missing-roll-electoral-commission-students-
block-individual-registration). There was no post-election comment
following this up. Why not?

On 3rd February 2015 the Huffington Post published an article called
One Million Voters Have Fallen Off Britain's Electoral Register
written by Paul Vale (see http://www.huffingtonpost.co.uk/
2015/02/02/one-million-voters-have-fallen-off-britains-electoral-
register_n_6600740.html

There was no post-election follow-up in the Guardian to Paul
Wheeler's comment on Thursday 5 February 2014 under the headline
"Britain's missing voters: why individual registration has been a
disaster"(see http://www.theguardian.com/public-leaders-network/
2015/feb/05/missing-voters-individual-electoral-registration-
disaster). Why not?

On May 8th 2015 the Huffington Post published an article on *the
General Election Pollsters To Conduct Enquiry Into Why They Were
So Wrong. (see* www.huffingtonpost.co.uk/2015/05/08/general-
election-polls-enquiry_n_7244892.html) It will be interesting to see
what they these pollsters can conclude without mentioning the
gerrymandering involved in the 2013 IER Act.

On 1st June 2015 The Guardian published an article called *What if
David Cameron is an evil genius?* written by Frankie Boyle (see

http://www.theguardian.com/commentisfree/2015/jun/01/david-cameron-moriarty-downing-street-radical-thatcher)

There were few such comments after the election, bar one: the Telegraph article on the early hours of 8 May, immediately after the Conservative victory, about the intended redrawing of constituency boundaries.

The newspapers and magazines which one might have expected, on the basis of their previous publication of about the flaws in the implementation of the 2013 IER Act - such as the Guardian, and the Huffington Post- did not provide post-election comment about the role of the IER in delivering a surprise Conservative victory.

For the largely foreign-owned press to fail to report on political events in the UK is par for the course. For the Guardian, the Independent and the New Statesman to fail to comment adequately on the reasons for the surprising Conservative victory on 7 May 2015 is remarkable.

It was almost as if there was the Government had issued a D-notice banning comment on the relationship between the Conservative win and the 2013 IER Act, although the previous three Guardian articles spelled out what their authors regarded as that relationship.

But the Guardian had had many long legal tussles with the Government in previous decades and perhaps the editor of that newspaper had no wish to face up to the possibility of another.

The BBC and ITV were both silent on the possible relationship between the change in the voting system the loss of voters, and how that affected the 2015 General Election. The BBC probably did not wish to antagonise its paymaster and ITV probably did not wish to run any programme its advertisers might not like. The BBC Parliament Channel ran a programme on Thursday 14 May 2015 asking "Who Won the UK General Election, How and Why?" introduced by Sir David Butler, Emeritus Fellow, Nuffield College, Oxford; featuring Sir Andrew Dilnot, the Warden of Nuffield College, Dr May Even, the Chair/Reuters institute for the Study of Journalism, Oxford University; Professor Geoff Evans, a Fellow of Nuffield College, Oxford; Professor Jane Green, Professor of Political Science of the University of Manchester, and a Co-Director of the 2015 British Election Study; and Peter Kellner, the President of YouGov, an organisation which describes itself as not partisan. All of these people, who one might expect to be tolerably well informed, got through the programme without once mentioning effect of the 2013 IER Act on the election. YouGov's internet polling methods may now be more accurate because the persons missing in the internet - the poor, the underprivileged, the BAME community, Council tenants and relocaters, and women - may reflect those absent in the 2013 IER voters register.

When the crisis in our democracy arrived, it seemed as if its press defenders had melted away and its informed commentators were all at sea, either because they really did not know what had happened or because they would lose research or Government funding if they told the truth.

I sent a copy of an article about about Conservative gerrymandering to the editors of the *New Statesman*, who I thought might be interested in that issue and who might consider printing it. They were not. Just as surprisingly, the reporters and editors of *HeraldScotland* were not interested.

The most important political development in 2015 undoubtedly was the election of the David Cameron Government against all the pollsters' predictions and the implementation by that Government of the most significantly destructive ultra-right-wing political programmes for the destruction of the British welfare state, the privatisation of the NHS and the planned 2016 gerrymandering of British constituencies to provide a Conservative future for decades.

These are historic events. It is obvious that in any contest between the electorate and the Government that the Government is unstoppable if it chooses to gerrymander the electoral rolls or the constituency boundaries. All power in the British parliamentary system tests with an elected government which can decide issues in its own partisan interest regardless of the protests put forward by the Electoral Commission, Parliament's Political and Constitutional Reform Committee, or any other minority political parties. There is no defence against political betrayal of the interests of the people by an elected government. The Political and Constitutional Reform

Committee published its report on 4 November 2011. As Isobel White's HoC Briefing Paper SNO6762 on IER reported on page 7:

"The Committee concluded that there was broad agreement on the principle of IER but very differing views on how it should be implemented.

The Committee recommended that the Government should reconsider its decision not to hold a full household canvass in 2014 [because]:

'We have heard serious concerns that the Government's current proposals will miss an unacceptably large number of potential electors, and calls from many of our witnesses for a full household canvass in 2014 to address this problem. We believe, given the unique circumstances of the change to IER, that the Government should reconsider its decision not to hold a full household canvass in 2014. The Committee also recommended that it should initially be an offence to fail to complete a voter registration form although this could be reviewed after five years of operation of the new system 'by which time registration levels may be high enough and a culture of individual registration sufficiently embedded for compulsion no longer to be necessary'."

Needless to say, the Government did not alter its view to hold no household canvass in 2014. And the Electoral Commission commented (among other things) in a report dated 23 October 2013 on the results of the Government's test of the CLR match rates that

"• However, match rates varied from 46.9% in Kensington and Chelsea to 86.4% in Mansfield.

• Students, young adults and private renters were least likely to be automatically transferred."

That is no way to run a democracy but the Government rushed to judgement anyway. It is interesting to note that Parliament's Political and Constitutional Reform Committee thought the IER system could take five years to bed in.

The losers in the 2013 IER Act have consistently been identified as "Students, young adults and private renters". There are millions of these, and they mainly are non-Conservative voters. Given time - say the extra year to December 2016 - many of these voters would re-register under the IER system, but time was something the Government has no intention of giving them. Freezing the Parliamentary Electoral Rolls as a basis for redrawing constituency boundaries on a partisan basis was, for the Government, a much higher objective than giving more time to allow these voter registers to contain more non-Conservative voters. In June 2015 the Electoral Commission reported about the progress of the transition to the new system of IER and it did not recommend an early end to the transition period, suggesting the December 2016 completion date for the introduction of the first phase of IER should be retained.

The Government ignored this and on 16 July 2015 laid the Electoral Registration and Administration Act 2013 (Transitional Provisions) Order 2015 before Parliament. The Order will end the transition to IER in December 2015 instead of December 2016.

David Cameron's Government only consults its own partisan interests in deciding issues relating to voter registration and the 2013 IER Act. All the other consultations with and recommendations from other bodies are ignored if they conflict with the Government's partisan agenda.

**3.8 28th February 2015 'Osborne's Dream of the Continuation of Neoclassical Economics
Is "A Boot Stamping On Human Face Forever" 'By Bryan Gould and George Tait Edwards**

This article was originally published by Bryan Gould and George Tait Edwards on Saturday 28th February 2015 as the first section of a series of nine articles about the possible "Economic Policies for an Incoming Labour Government" in the London Progressive Journal at http://londonprogressivejournal.com/article/view/2122/economic-policies-for-an-incoming-labour-government-part-of and it was re-titled and republished on April 19th 2015 at https://medium.com/@georgetaitedwards/osborne-s-dream-of-the-continuation-of-neoclassical-economics-is-a-boot-stamping-on-human-face-c3d0b97a94f4

"1 The record of the Coalition Government beggars belief
In economic terms George Osborne's record is appalling. The so-called recovery has been delayed unnecessarily for more than half a decade and this means that a return to pre-2008 living standards is still many years away. Median GDP is still 3% below 2007 levels, and since the population has increased by 3%, that means an average fall in individual incomes of 6%. The decline of the productive sector and particularly of manufacturing has meant that only 10% of our GDP is now accounted for by manufacturing—the lowest proportion of any major developed economy—and our share of world trade has fallen to just 2.7%.

2 The disastrous fall in family incomes
Coalition polices have resulted in the sharpest fall in living standards in more than 60 years. According to data from the Institute of Fiscal Studies, average wages have fallen by over £1,600 since 2010, at an average rate of over £530 a year. The pre-Coalition reduction in median income (not the same as average wages, but an acceptable proxy), can be calculated at about £5,400 over thirty years (1980 to 2010)—about £180 a year—so that the Coalition has produced a reduction in worker incomes of almost three times the previous trend. But these figures relate only to the working population, and take no account of the reduction in unemployment and disability benefits, the denial of benefits to mothers seeking work because they have not

been employed during the previous two years, and the exclusion from the data for both the employed and unemployed of the growing practice of zero-hours contracts, all of which mean that the real extent of income cuts is much larger than official figures indicate. The burden imposed on working people has not of course been shared by the wealthiest people in our society. According to an Oxfam report [1] , the richest 5 families in Britain have more wealth than the poorest 20% of the population. That level of inequality is unprecedented since records began in the UK. In a more recent report [2] , Oxfam tells us that the Coalition's welfare cuts have pushed 1.75 million of the UK's poorest households deeper into poverty, suffering an absolute cut in their income in the past three years and leaving them struggling to cover food and energy bills.

And all the attendant evils of this unprecedented decline in working-class living standards are now manifest in Coalition Britain. The national scandal that millions of children in the UK are going to bed hungry is not some accidental by-product of Coalition policy. It is the inevitable and deliberate consequence of policies pursued by a government that is "of the privileged, by the privileged, for the privileged".

2 Coalition Targeting of the Disadvantaged and Women

The disadvantaged poor—the disabled, the sick and the unemployed —have suffered, through cuts in their benefits, the greatest burdens in dealing with the recession. SCOPE, the charity supporting disabled people, have shown, for example, that 600,000 people in the UK lost a total of £2.62 billion pounds a year from Monday 8 April 2013 as a result of the Coalition Government abolishing the Disability Living Allowance (DLA) and introducing the new Personal Independence Payment (PIP), with tighter eligibility criteria and a controversial new assessment. The purpose of that change is not to improve service or to make things more fair but simply to save money. The lack of concern for the most disadvantaged in our society was compounded by the amazingly (and deliberately) inaccurate statements about incapacity benefit made by Ian Duncan Smith. Coalition policies have disproportionately affected women, who are disproportionately found in lower-paid occupations and in the caring professions.

An analysis of Treasury data by House of Commons Library researchers in 2012 showed that £11.1bn of the £14.9bn raised from the five spending reviews since 2010 comes from women even though they earn less than men on average. Planned changes to tax credits, child benefits and public sector pensions were largely to blame. They came shortly after the government announced plans to cut the 50p top rate of tax for all those earning over £150,000. Guardian research has shown that the Conservative Party is 84% funded by 15 very rich people, 14 of them based in the City of London. The Conservative Party are proposing to stun the British electorate with that money in order to try to win an election they deserve to lose. If the person who pays the piper calls the tune, how can we ever expect the Conservative Party to run Britain in the interests of most of its people, and not just in the interests of the already rich and privileged? Could that funding explain why the Coalition Government have behaved as they have?

3 All of the Coalition's "Greatest Achievements" are Malign

What is the greatest achievement of the Conservative-led Coalition? Destroying the health service by setting NHS budgets well below the level of need? The creation of millions of starving families and children in Britain? Destroying the future prospects of a decent life for our children? The destruction of the social fabric by setting the budget for social benefits so low that many benefit entitlements cannot be paid? Training DWP staff to mislead the unemployed about the availability and the rights to benefits so as to stay within the reduced DWP allocated budget? Making the the poorest pay for the credit crunch caused by the banks and government economic incompetence? Prioritising tax cuts for the rich and creating an economic recovery with lower median incomes? All of these things they have done, and they promise much more of the same, only worse, if they are re-elected to power.

4 Neoclassical Economics Has No Future

The budget day picture painted by Gilbert George Osborne of Britain's future is totally bleak. A Britain without an NHS, a future in which the credit squeeze chases real living standards further down indefinitely in order to reduce taxes for his paymasters, the already stinking rich. Does anyone except Osborne and Cameron believe they can cut median incomes, already down by £7,000 since 1980, by further thousands of pounds in all the years to come? Do they imagine the British will put up with declining living standards and

interminable attacks on the poor and underprivileged indefinitely?
The compliant British media have ignored street protests against the
government, but the levels of repression that would be needed to
enforce further steep reductions in British living standards have not
so far featured in, or been proposed by, any government programme.

5 Conclusion

Osborne's vision of the future of Britain is "A boot stamping on a
human face forever."
That's what he wants to do, and what neoclassical economics
justifies.
Nobody sensible should vote for that."

And a majority of the electorate didn't.

3.9 How David Cameron's Government Stole the 2015 General Election The two major electoral rolls - the Local Authority Electoral Roll and the Parliamentary Electoral Roll - are both meant to be an objective list of all the eligible electors. These rolls of qualifying British electors were, prior to the 2013 IER Act, based mainly upon the annual Household Electoral Review which, by post in each year, requested the 20 million householders to list accurately the qualifying residents occupying each house on a due date. The penalty for the head of the household not accurately filling in and returning the form was £1,000. New voters resident in the house - these "attainers" who were 17 and about to become 18 and qualified to vote within a year - were also listed on the return. Universities were similarly requested to return a list of all their students.

The 2013 IER Act is entirely different and has ten major elements which might be individually be defended but taken together clearly show how the implementation of that Act deletes voters, makes voter registration more difficult than previous, and blames voters for their non-registration and political apathy when it is the chosen Government implementation of that Act which is at fault.

First, the continual bias towards voter deletion rather than maximising voter numbers

The historical drive of the Electoral Commission and the 348 Electoral Registration Officers in England has previously been towards maximising the number of eligible voters on the Electoral Rolls, in the interests of establishing representative democracy on the widest possible basis. The bias exercised in the Coalition and Conservative implementation of the 2013 IER has been entirely partisan and focused upon reducing those voters who are unlikely to vote Conservative on the Electoral Rolls. The best example of this is university students, who often had (and perhaps a few still have) two entries on the Parliamentary Electoral Roll - one at their term-time address and one at their home address. Now 920,000 students in England now have neither. The cry from some Conservative Party Members is that students have disenfranchised themselves by their laziness, because if each student had filled in the forms allegedly given to them on the day of their University registration, then they might not have been deleted from the voting rolls. But it as not their laziness which removed them from the rolls, but deliberate partisan

Government action which required action by these potential voters rather than automatic registration based on the previous Household Electoral Registration (HER) System.

Second, when an IER system was introduced in the Northern Ireland after 2002, there was a 10.5% drop in the voter registers. As page 4 of the House of Commons Library Briefing Paper Number 6764, authored by Isobel White and dated 21 July 2015, notes

"When individual registration was introduced in Northern Ireland by the Electoral Fraud (Northern Ireland) Act 2002, the numbers on the register there fell by 10.5% although the legislation was seen as successful in reducing electoral fraud."

But minor levels of fraud were possibly eliminated at the cost of the disenfranchisement of hundreds of thousands of electors - a massive loss to the democratic process in Northern Ireland.

The British Government knew that the introduction of the 2013 IER Act, if implemented as it was in Northern Ireland, would lead to a large fall in voter registration.

The Irish troubles began, according to most analyses, because the Irish Authorities gerrymandered the outcome of the elections in a blatant denial of the democratic process. Whatever the stated objectives of the 2002 Electoral Fraud (Northern Ireland) Act the result is the re-establishment of the gerrymandering, this time by Westminster rather than by local politicians. The gerrymandering in this Act therefore once again provides the conditions on the ground for the resurgence of the Troubles which Mo Mowlem's 1998 Easter Sunday Agreement had briefly laid to rest. Again on Page 4 [the first *Background*] paragraph of that briefing paper

"The [Electoral]Commission published a report in June 2003, *Voting for change: an electoral law modernisation programme,* which brought together recommendations from a series of policy papers, including those on registration issues. The Labour Government responded to the report in 2004 and said it was sympathetic to the principles of individual registration but it did not implement the

Commission's recommendations, mainly because of concerns about the effect on levels of registration if a system of individual registration was introduced."

The Labour Party knew that a badly-implemented individual elector registration system would damage democracy by creating large levels of voter under-registration. These under-registered voters were mainly labour voters - students, tenants of local authority housing, ethnic minorities - so Labour had a sound democratic reason as well as a political reason for not wishing to progress this process. But the Conservative Party had no similar qualms and, as events have demonstrated, had no reservations about damaging the British democratic process if it suited their partisan objectives.

Third, the use of only one government database - the DWP one - to confirm electors

The British Government has at its disposal dozens of databases about British citizens. If there had been a genuine intention to re-establish the Parliamentary Electoral Rolls by identifying all legitimate voters in the United Kingdom, the Government could have used several of the Government's voluminous databases to ensure that virtually all potential voters were entered on the rolls. Instead, only one database - the Department of Work and Pensions one - was used to establish a baseline of potential voters.

There is a motor insurance database which records the insurance of 47 million vehicles. There is an HMRC database which has the details of 29.7 million individual income tax payers. There is the Passport Agency which lists about 80% of the UK population who have a passport. There is a National Insurance database which contains a record of every person over 16 in the United Kingdom. As the Wikipedia entry records "In order to administer the National Insurance system, a National Insurance number is allocated to every child in the United Kingdom shortly before their 16th birthday" (see https://en.wikipedia.org/wiki/National_Insurance).

The UK is estimated to have had a population of about 64.6 million in 2014. (See https://en.wikipedia.org/wiki/Demography_of_the_United_Kingdom#Age_structure). About 11 million were under 14 in 2011 and a further 4 million were 15-19, so the over 19 population looks likely to be about 50 million and the over 18 population about 50.8 millions. A complete UK voters roll would therefore be in excess of 50 million if all the relevant databases were used to identify all the legal electorate in the UK. The DWP database only contains 42.4 million records, much less than the December 2013 electoral roll which identified 46.2 million voters. The DWP records used in the "Confirmation Live Run" for England and Wales initially identified voters from the DWP database only produced a voters' roll of 36.9 million voters with 5.5 million voters not confirmed, so initially disenfranchised these 5.5 million voters - 13% of the electorate - an even larger percentage loss than 10.5% reduction in voters in Northern Ireland.

As section 3.5 above illustrates, in a comparison of the Australian Implementation of IER with the Cameron-led Coalition Government's implementation of the 2013 IER Act, a government can maximise voter registration by using all the databases at its disposal. Successive Australian Governments have done that, the Cameron-led Coalition and Conservative governments have chosen not to do that.

Fourth, The abolition of the 2014 HER/Annual canvass
The abolition of the 2014 Household Electoral Review (HER) was a deliberate decision of the Coalition Government removed the possibility of correcting the flawed early 2014 IER Act register by writing to the missing electors. It is impossible to conclude that this was not a deliberate partisan act to minimise non-Conservative voters.

Fifth, the absence of ring-fencing of the money provided to improve the Parliamentary Electoral Register (PER)
The Coalition Government did provide two tranches of funds in February 2015 to improve voter registration on the PER but these funds were not earmarked for that specific purpose. The result of this was that many cash-strapped local authorities in the UK used the money provided to maintain essential services instead of improving voter registration. If the Coalition Government had been serious about improving the PER it would have ring-fenced these funds for their stated purpose.

Sixth, the denial of the suggestion that voters could register on voting day at the booths
Several countries that have introduced IER legislation have allowed voters to present identity information at the voting booths on polling

day, so that they could vote despite not being previously registered. That suggestion was made by Sadiq Khan the deputy leader of the opposition but was ignored by the Government.

It is difficult not to conclude that the Government had no wish to allow voters which had been disenfranchised by the 2013 IER or otherwise unregistered voters to vote on polling day.

Seventh, the refusal to consider the issues raised by the Electoral Commission

During the implementation of the 2013 IER Act the Electoral Commission (EC) continually issued suggestions about how the Act could be better implemented. For example, the EC suggested that the 2014 HER should be held to improve voter registration and that the completion date of the IER implementation should remain December 2016 as planned in the original timetable of IER introduction. The Government ignored all such suggestions and abolished the 2014 IER and rushed to complete the IER implementation by December 2015. These actions ensured that the PER was less complete than it would be if the Electoral Commission recommendations had been introduced, and paved the way for a less complete PER to be used as the basis for the planned gerrymandering of constituency boundaries (which was planned, on the basis of that a reduced PER, to lock in Conservative Majority governments for generations). See the announcement made hours after the Conservative victory on http://www.telegraph.co.uk/news/11593496/New-Commons-boundaries-top-Conservative-government-agenda.html.

Eighth, the voting down of parliamentary motions criticising the fast implementation of the 2013 IER Act

Several Early Day Motions were proposed and voted upon in The House of Commons to improve the number of voters being registered in the PER under the provisions of the 2013 IER Act. All of these were voted down by the Government majority in the interests of minimising the number of voters on the PER. These votes produced the flawed PER used on polling day and the flawed mandate of a 7th May 2015 General Election.

Ninth, the reduction of the penalty for non-responses to a request for voter registration from a likely £1,000 on the previous HER system to a weak comment on the IER Enquiry forms about how

"You might be fined £80".
The lowering of the penalty for non-responses and the
encouragement of non-registration of an individual's voting rights
acts to produce a flawed PER which advantages the Conservative
Party.

**Tenth, the Cameron Government proposes to use the reduced
and gerrymandered 2013 IER Act Parliamentary Electoral Roll
produced in early 2015 as the basis for the gerrymandering of
constituency boundaries in 2016 with the objective of locking in
Conservative Governments for generations.**

See the press announcement reported in the Daily Telegraph on 8
May 2015 a few hours after the election of the Cameron-led
Conservative Government which states that one objective of the new
parliamentary boundaries is to gerrymander Conservative victories
for generations.

See http://www.telegraph.co.uk/news/11593496/New-Commons-
boundaries-top-Conservative-government-agenda.html which is
discussed in more detail in Section 4.1 below.

There can be no doubt whatsoever that IER Act 2013 Coalition
gerrymander has been the major factor in "electing" the extreme
right wing Cameron Conservative Government on 7 May 2015.

All of the pollsters' predictions one month before the 7 May General
Election election showed a hung parliament, yet the exit polls
showed the Conservatives might be 10 short of an overall majority.
The opinion polls all asked samples of supposed voters about voting
intentions, while the exit polls recorded how voters who could vote
had voted.

The Tories had 11,334,576 votes in total, 36.9% of the voters, and
330 seats. Labour had 9,347,304 votes, 30.4% of the voters, and 256
seats. The turnout was 66% and the Conservative majority appeared
to be 1,987,272 votes. Compared with the polls, which had predicted
about 305 seats for the Conservatives, a surplus 25 seats turned up
for the Conservatives, with a working majority of 12. Wikipedia

reported without any trace of irony that

"Opinion polls were eventually proven to have significantly underestimated the Conservative vote, which bore resemblance to their surprise victory in the 1992 general election."

and, I would add, for the same gerrymandering reasons - by the Poll Tax in 1992 and the 2013 IER Act in 2015.

See https://en.wikipedia.org/wiki/
United_Kingdom_general_election,_2015#Opinion_polling_inaccura
cies_and_scrutiny

Calculations comparing the 2015 election results with the one month previous polls suggest that the 2013 IER has produced about 1.8 million missing Labour voters.

Cameron's Tories won 24% support of the alleged total electorate and 36% of those who voted. No matter how these numbers are manipulated, the Conservatives have no grass roots support in the UK, and they certainly do not have a popular democratic mandate for the enormous changes they are implementing. There is no popular mandate whatsoever for the destruction of the third pillar of the post war consensus - the welfare state - or for the privatisation of the NHS.

These plans will make the Tories a toxic political brand. The Conservatives would never hold office again if they did not have plans further to gerrymander the electoral process, but they have such plans, as section 4.1 reports.

3.10 11 June 2015 "Has David Cameron Committed Misconduct While in Public Office?"

This very short article was first published on 11th June 2015 at https://medium.com/@georgetaitedwards/has-david-cameron-committed-misconduct-while-in-public-office-8542a018fbe8

'"Misconduct While in Public Office" is defined by the Crown Prosecution Service (see http://www.cps.gov.uk/legal/l_to_o/misconduct_in_public_office/) as
"The elements of misconduct in public office are:
a) A public officer acting as such.
b) Wilfully neglects to perform his duty and/or wilfully misconducts himself.
c) To such a degree as to amount to an abuse of the public's trust in the office holder.
d) Without reasonable excuse or justification."
Is it possible that David Cameron MP, acting as the highest public officer, has wilfully misconducted himself to gerrymander the Electoral Roll to such a degree as to amount to an abuse of the public's trust in the office he holds, without reasonable excuse or justification, except for his personal objective of retaining his post as Prime Minister and his partisan objective of winning the 2015 General Election on the basis of a gerrymandered electoral roll?
What do you think?
Gerrymandering does not seem to be illegal in the United Kingdom but the Prime Minister using government of the day to fix the electoral rolls looks like misconduct in public office to me.
Should David Cameron be indicted for that offence?
Please form an orderly queue.'

It seems very likely to me that the disgraceful actions of David Cameron - in placing into the statute book the 2013 IER Act which has disenfranchised millions of voters and thus gerrymandered the 2015 election to produce a Conservative "win" - has committed misconduct while in public office. If David Cameron were an American President he would be impeached for that activity.

But this is England, where there is more lenient leeway for very bad behaviour by a rich member of the privileged upper class.

4 The Future

This chapter focuses upon the next three stages of Conservative gerrymandering relating to the 2013 IER Act and presents three articles contrasting the approach of the Conservative Government with the economics practised in the Tokyo consensus zone. An Anti-austerity UK budget is suggested and the macroeconomics of the Tokyo Consensus Zone is set out in sections 4.6 to 4.9. Finally this chapter suggests how a fully representative democracy could be re-established in the UK.

4.1 David Cameron's plan for a one-party state in the future of England

There are three aspects to David Cameron's plan to progress the results of the 2013 IER Act into a semi-permanent advantage to the Conservative party. These are:

a) Finishing the introduction phase of the 2013 IER Act by December 2015 (a year earlier than the original schedule)
b) Disenfranchising up to seven million voters currently on the Parliamentary Electoral register if they do not respond to the letters sent to them by December 2015, and
c) Gerrymandering the constituency boundaries to the advantage of the Conservatives by loading missing and mainly non-Conservative voters into constituencies based upon the reduced number of IER voters

The rush to judgement and the finishing the introduction phase of the 2013 IER Act by December 2015 instead of December 2016 is probably motivated by three main considerations. First, the Government is anxious to end discussion about the flawed procedures used in implementing the 2013 IER Act and wishes to close off any further objection by making what it has done into an historical fact. Second, the one-year earlier closure of the implantation phase of the 2013 IER Act stops currently pending and additional activities which might result in more voters registering, and makes the December 2015 deadline for additional voter registration an end piece of the Act, freezing voter numbers as a basis for what adjusting constituency boundaries. And third, the Cameron

Government wishes to pursue its stated highest priority - the use of the flawed and frozen 2013 IER Act Parliamentary Voter Registration data in December 2015 - for a 2016 gerrymandering of constituency boundaries which, the Government has announced "may lock Labour out of power for decades," as the Telegraph pointed out at 5.36 am on 8 May 2015, on the morning after the General Election under the heading "New Commons boundaries top Conservative government agenda" - see

http://www.telegraph.co.uk/news/11593496/New-Commons-boundaries-top-Conservative-government-agenda.html

This article begins

"Redrawing constituency boundaries to lock Labour out of power for decades is at the top of the agenda for the new Conservative government, senior Tories have said.The changes to parliamentary boundaries, blocked in the last Parliament, could be confirmed quickly and take effect at the 2020 general election, party sources suggested."

And how will this redrawing take place? It will be conducted in 2016 and based on the reduced number of Parliamentary voters produced by the 2013 IER Act. The article continues by pointing out that the effect of the change in constituency boundaries is likely to be an almost-permanent Conservative Government "for decades." The intention in the redrawing of these boundaries is to trap non-Conservative voters in a minority of seats and to jury-rig the boundaries to prevent any resurgence of voters producing a non-Conservative government. That objective is profoundly undemocratic, but I understand there are computer programmes which can reallocate each voting ward to produce that result.

The Telegraph report on that intention is unique. No other newspaper or media outlet has carried that story. The "glory" of a gerrymandered Conservative victory seems to have caused an amazing burst of honesty about the gerrymandering intentions of Cameron and his party. It is of course natural for the reporters of the Telegraph - the major British broadsheet which has constantly supported the Conservatives in all circumstances - to ask this "just-elected" Conservative Government "What is their highest priority?" The Conservatives' spokesmen who advised the Telegraph seem to have blown their fuses in their early hours of glory and answered with an unusual frankness. Their stated highest priority is to prevent their Labour opponents from holding office for decades.

As the Telegraph report says:

"The projections show that the Tories would have gained 314 seats if the new boundaries had been passed before the election. That would be 52.3 per cent of the Commons. The Tories gained 50.9 per cent of MPs under the current system.
Labour would have gained 211 out of the 600 seats. This is 35.1 per cent of the proposed 600 seats, while it won 35.7 per cent of the 650 seats currently in Parliament."

So the Cameron-led Conservatives plan to gerrymander constituency boundaries on top of the gerrymandered 2013 IER Act Parliamentary Electoral Roll to produce a landslide for the Conservatives in the 2020 election and to prevent Labour from ever holding office during the 2020s and 2030s and maybe even in the 2040s. David Cameron's Conservative Government, implementing right-wing policies for which he has a gerrymandered 2015 Conservative victory, plans to further fix future elections for decades much more thoroughly than he fixed the 2015 one.

These figures giving the number of seats in the new boundaries are curiously precise. Perhaps the Conservative Party HQ in Smith Square has already run a computer simulation with altered constituencies. There are no error margins quoted around the seat numbers, which is unusual for such predictions. I have calculated that on the basis of the Telegraph data the Conservatives could form a parliamentary majority with only 20% of the full electorate voting for that party. That isn't democracy!

In the light of that Telegraph report, the views of Peter Facey, from Unlock Democracy, (quoted in section 3.4 page 1) seem prescient. He linked the drop in voter numbers caused by the implementation of the 2013 IER Act with "the ongoing review of parliamentary boundaries" and commented that "the connection is problematic given the close proximity in terms of timings." He referred to the view that "the timing of IER taken together with the boundary review could give rise to the perception that the reforms were motivated by partisan interests. As a result, some participants supported the view that either the introduction of IER or boundary review should be delayed."

Of course neither have been delayed. It is now nearly impossible to deny the view that the reforms "were motivated by partisan interests". Once the British people realise this, how acceptable will such behaviour become?

The British people have a long and honourable tradition of extending the democratic mandate. The Conservatives would probably have had some difficulty in winning the 2015 General Election if their platform was "We've gerrymandered the Parliamentary Electoral Rolls to guarantee our victory, no matter how you vote, and we are going to gerrymander the constituency boundaries after we get in."

The Conservative Party throughout history have constantly opposed and voted against these increases in the numbers of voters. The Conservative Party have voted against extending the mandate to more adult males, against votes for women, against votes for the young. In modern decades the votes for sixteen to eighteen year olds has been implemented in Scotland but not in England and Wales.

I think the final outcome of the Cameron-led Conservative gerrymandering, aiming at the control of parliament for decades, is extremely likely to have other unplanned effects, as will be considered in Section 5.1.

Prime Minister David Cameron, like his Chancellor Gideon (call me George) Oliver Osborne, both assume an economic competence that neither possesses. The best way to illustrate that is by comparing David Cameron with Japan's great Prime Minister Shinzo Abe (in section 4.2), and by setting out how George Osborne's 2013 Budget Speech might have been (in Section 4.3) if he understood the growth-maximising inflation-limiting much more successful version of macroeconomics practised in the Tokyo Consensus Zone.

4.2 First September 2013 - "A Tale of Two Prime Ministers: David Cameron the Neo-classical vs Shinzo Abe the Shimomuran"

This article was first published on first September 2013 at http://londonprogressivejournal.com/article/view/1585/a-tale-of-two-prime-ministers and was re-published on July 19th 2014 at https://medium.com/@georgetaitedwards/a-tale-of-two-prime-ministers-cdb326b5f6c3

"1 A Difference in Vision
On 19 April 2013, in a speech to the Japan National Press Club, Shinzo Abe set out his vision for the future of the Japanese economy and he outlined part of his personal philosophy, his political policies and his proposed government's activities which all are aimed at improving the prospects and prosperity of all the Japanese people within the next ten years. You can read that speech at

http://www.kantei.go.jp/foreign/96_abe/statement/201304/19speech_e.html

David Cameron has never set out his vision of Britain's future in similar precise terms. He has of course voiced the usual platitudes that he is a "modern compassionate conservative" but his political activity and legislative programme are best described as an old-fashioned, callous and more extreme form of Thatcherism. Apart from that self-description, there appears to be no comparable and coherent statement of Cameron's personal philosophy, nor any such statement about any future political policies or government activity aimed at improving the prosperity of the British people.

That is a great pity because a comparison between the two men is inevitably a contrast between the powerful and active presence of Shinzo Abe, and his detailed political and economic proposals to improve Japan's economic future, and the absence, inaction on major crises and silence of David Cameron on most of these issues.

Inevitably, Cameron appears to respond to individual issues without the assistance of any overall vision. For example, on the issue of low pay, John Sentamu, the Archbishop of York, has said in an Observer article dated 20 July 2013 entitled "The Scandal of MIllions not Paid Enough to Live On" that Cameron is "offering only platitudes when addressing the problem." See the report at

http://www.theguardian.com/society/2013/jul/20/john-sentamu-living-wage-scandal

John Sentamu also raises several related issues which will further illustrate the comparison between the two Prime Ministers, as commented upon below. In the following sections, I will use the major headings of the Shinzo Abe speech and some of the relevant points of Sentamu's article as a framework for comparisons.

2.1 Shinzo Abe's introduction to his policies

As President of the Liberal Democratic Party, Shinzo Abe became the Japanese Prime Minister for the second time on 16 December 2012. As the Wikipedia entry reads:

"In elections on 16 December 2012, the LDP won 294 seats in the 480 seat lower house of parliament. Following his victory, Abe said "With the strength of my entire cabinet, I will implement bold monetary policy, flexible fiscal policy and a growth strategy that encourages private investment and, with these three policy pillars, achieve results""Abenomics, as his economic policy has been called, consists of fiscal and monetary expansion with a 2% target interest rate."

See http://en.wikipedia.org/wiki/Shinz%C5%8D_Abe

Shinzo Abe began his speech by telling the story of Ino Tadataka, who from the age of 55 (at a time when Japanese life expectancy was 50) travelled all over Japan, covering over 40,000 km, and producing excellent maps. Shinzo Abe draws the life-lesson from Tadataka's example, that

"No matter how difficult a challenge may seem, it is always possible to overcome it provided you have a strong will never to give up-.There is no such thing as "too late" to take action."

Shinzo Abe's growth strategy encompasses both monetary and fiscal policy as summarised above and outlined below. Mr Abe mentioned several issues - the urgent need to deal with the disaster area around the Fukushima nuclear reactor by creating a Reconstruction Agency and removing the hindrances to reconstruction; prolonged deflation, which the target of 2% inflation, agreed by the Bank of Japan and the Government, should remedy; education in crisis, which specific actions could help remedy; damaged Japanese diplomacy, which has been improved by visits establishing better international relations; and the provocations from North Korea, which would be best dealt with within the wider international context by a unified message to North Korea from the USA, the Republic of Korea, China and Russia.

2.2 Higher pay for workers - from Shinzo Abe's introduction

Shinzo Abe has the national objective of paying Japanese workers as much as possible.

As he says:

"With the passage of the supplementary budget, flexible fiscal policy is also now moving into the stage of execution. In order to enable the fruits of these endeavours to reach the people as quickly as possible, I myself have made direct requests to industrial circles that they raise workers' pay by the greatest amount possible. The tax system also supports companies that return profits to their employees.

In this year's spring labour offensive, a number of companies decided to raise employees' remuneration, including statements that bonuses would be paid in full."

By contrast, David Cameron's policy is not only to reduce the benefits of the unemployed but also to keep low the earnings of the employed by maintaining the indefensible minimum wage legislation and through higher taxation. Cameron has not asked the CBI to try to persuade British Companies to pay a living wage, and the idea that he might ever do so, given his known attitudes, seems unlikely.

As John Sentamu, Archbishop of York, pointed out in his Observer article:

"The scale of low pay in Britain is a national scandal. Come pay day, nearly five million people in this country won't have been paid at a rate high enough to live on. Just think about that. Nearly five million people give their time, their skills and their energy to perform jobs – many of which we all depend on – but don't get paid enough by their employers to even get by. That means not enough money to heat their homes, or feed their families, or plan for a rainy day."

The Coalition government, who have directly attacked the welfare of the unemployed, the disabled and the poor, have neither a policy nor any programme to improve the prosperity of British workers.

2.3 Shinzo Abe's three Three Key Words - challenges, openness, innovation

Shinzo Abe proposes a 2% inflation target for the BoJ, along with a 2% interest rate on credit, so the Japanese can continue their historical policy of trying to set the interest rate equal to the inflation rate (which is the economic condition for the maximisation of real wealth by making borrowed money a counterpart of real resources - see section 8 of

http://londonprogressivejournal.com/article/view/1497/shimomuran-economics-the-nodebt-investment-credit-creation-path-to-more-rapid-economic-growth.

Shinzo Abe's Japan of the future will have "Abundant capital, directed to growth areas, removing funding obstacles"

The Coalition government, by contrast, has cut the public works capital programme in nearly all areas. The cuts in local authority budgets and in quango budgets have so far been very severe. Now, in the run-up to the next election, the Coalition Government are desperately trying to produce a private and public sector building boom so as to improve their chances of being re-elected. This is working to a limited extent in the housing construction sector but not in the public sector. The staff that once implemented the higher investment public sector programmes (for example in the "Schools and colleges for the Future" programmes) are no longer there in sufficient numbers to implement any major buildings growth programme. The newly promised public sector higher funds are only an increase until the date of the next election, after which the temporary rise in capital funding falls down a cliff again. And the funds must be spent in-year, which can never be guaranteed for capital projects. All in all, the government's lately found enthusiasm for a quick electoral fix through more public building projects cannot work because, like so many Coalition activities, it is very amateurish, and their budget cuts have damaged the previously-existing implementation process.

And in my view, the cuts have been too deep and the damage to so many families has been too great, for any capital funds "sticking plaster" to reverse their standing at the polls.

The British Coalition Government have no intention of adopting the Abe policies - no policy of providing abundant capital, directing it to growth areas in the economy, and removing funding obstacles. And the current British Government have no understanding whatsoever of wealth creation using the Shimomuran investment credit economics within which Shinzo Abe's policies are framed.

2.4 Shinzo Abe - "Activate all Japanese Human Resources, Especially Women"

Shinzo Abe said: '"Women participating actively in society" is something that tends to be mentioned in the context of social policy. However, I see it quite differently. I view it as forming the central core of my Growth Policy.

I firmly believe that enabling women's latent high degree of ability to blossom fully will be a driving force that puts Japan, which has had the feeling of being caught in an impasse, on a growth track once more."

The Cameron Coalition Government has no such policy - quite the contrary.

So the greater participation of all human resources and a proper and more equal role for women is a central plank of Shinzo Abe's policy, as opposed to the undermining of women's independence through the low-pay-policies of the Coalition government, and the absence of any UK political programme to give women the social and economic positions their talents justify.

Shinzo Abe also sees the need for greater innovation and intellectual property.

Cameron doesn't see the need for either, and even if he did, he would be disinclined to do anything about it.

Shinzo Abe intends to assist international stability through international visits and economic diplomacy - through playing a full part in the Trans-Pacific Policy of co-operation with the USA, and through meetings with Russia and Middle East governments, especially the UAE.

Cameron's major focus is on the possible withdrawal of the UK from the great project of a United Europe, and the possible dissolution of the United Kingdom, largely brought about by the Scottish response to Thatcher's use of Scotland as a early test bed for the Poll tax and privatisation policies. As the commentators on "Not the Nine O'-Clock News" have remarked, there are more pandas in Scotland than Conservative MPs.

The Coalition Government behaves more like an elected dictatorship than an elected government. Policies developed in the darkness of Smith Square by the Conservative Party are then sprung upon the electorate as government policy despite the absence of any commitment to that policy during the election.

The Coalition-enforced privatisation of the NHS, despite Cameron's promise that the NHS would be "Safe in his hands", is but one example of that.

On nearly all the Coalition issues - the bedroom tax, the attacks on the living standards of the poor and disabled, and the real-terms cuts in unemployment allowances - the Coalition government is victimising the groups which it believes to be largely labour supporters. That is extremely divisive, compared to Shinzo Abe's commitment to involve all Japanese people in his growth plans.

2.5 Shinzo Abe's Policy that Growth Industries Are To Be Created from a "Society of Good Health and Longevity"
These proposals include a major focus on healthcare and medical technology, the creation of "Medical Excellence, Japan", with 110bn Yen for IPS Cell Research, investment in Automated Cell Sheet Technology, the formation of innovation-accelerating research clusters and structures, and the copying of the US NIH structures in Japan.

Shinzo Abe quotes the Illustrative example of a letter from a disabled girl:

"The other day, I received a letter from a girl who graduated from elementary school this year. She was born with an intractable illness by which her small intestine fails to function and she has not had a typical meal since she was very young. She has had surgery eight times already.

Her letter closed with the following line, expressing her expectations for IPS cell research:

"If a treatment can be found, then the future will be extremely bright. And I would love to be able to eat anything I like."

'It is also the responsibility and the role of politics to listen carefully and respond to wee voices such as hers, as she tries to live life with hope and a positive attitude."

Cameron doesn't seem to listen to anyone except the other members of his Eton-dominated Cabinet. If this young lady were in the United Kingdom, she might perhaps have been denied or delayed treatment on cost grounds, and the ATOS review might perhaps even have assessed her as a work-shy shirker, suitable for work.
Shinzo Abe continues:

"In particular, as someone who recovered from an intractable illness to once again become Prime Minister, I have a responsibility that can also be called my "destiny," to advance policies that take into account the perspective of people suffering from intractable illnesses.

"As soon as the "Japanese version of the NIH" is established, I wish to move straight into accelerating research on intractable illnesses as a national project. By doing so, I will work to create a society in which even people suffering from intractable illnesses at present can have hope for the future.

"This is what a "society of good health and longevity" should be like. I will move forward in this endeavor as one of the pillars of my Growth Strategy that will lead to new industries."

Cameron's Coalition Government have no comparable policy.

2.6 Shinzo Abe wants "Participation by all"

In Section 4 (entitled A Growth Strategy That Enjoys Participation by All) of Shinzo Abe's speech, Abe refers to Dr Osamu Shimomura as follows:

"Dr.Osamu Shimomura, who set forth the theory of the "income doubling plan" during Japan's period of high growth, said in a paper entitled "The Possibilities and Conditions for Economic Growth" that growth policy is the creation of "conditions that will bring into play to the greatest extent possible the capabilities actually held by the Japanese people."

"Dr.Shimomura pointed out that 45 million persons in the labour force had "few opportunities to demonstrate" their creative abilities "even though they have extremely high levels of latent ability" and explained that the Japanese economy would be able to grow only if these "opportunities" were provided properly."

I consider Dr. Shimomura's words to have universal value even now." In order to bring about higher Japanese growth, Mr Abe proposes "The movement of labour without unemployment" and " Better funding for higher skills re-training" and he further comments:

"It will be necessary to enhance workers' competencies in order to meet the needs of growth industries. We will considerably increase subsidies to support the movement of labour. These will help corporations that accept workers to cover the costs of training that are incurred."

No such programmes exist in the UK. The linkage which once existed in identifying industrial training needs and providing these was destroyed by the abolition of the Learning and Skills Council and the RDAs. Their replacement by Local Enterprise Partnerships may have saved a little money but the knowledge and experience lost in that process will take years, possibly decades, to recover. With the destruction of the Regional Development Agencies (RDAs) as the potential engines supporting regional economic growth, the responsibility for economic development has been centralised on the national government of Britain - a responsibility which the Coalition is woefully ill-equipped to deliver.

2.7 The creation of internationally competitive young people

Mr Abe proposes more Asian Exchange students, along with an emphasis on the learning of English so that different Asian nationalities can talk to one another in English, and he proposes a retimed, re-scheduled job application schedule within the year, to

help place returning overseas-studying Japanese on an even
recruitment basis with domestic
Japanese in job competition.

2.8 A Japan in which women shine versus a Britain in which many women are trapped in low-paid jobs which pay less than a living wage

Again, Shinzo Abe sets out his objectives in detail - for 30% of
Japanese leaders to be female, for the improvement of childcare ava-
iability via the "Yokohama Method" (of company-run nurseries) and
for better funding for childcare company start-ups.

By way of contrast, John Sentamu comments on the Cameron-led
Coalition's continuation of legally-set very low pay (below the cost
of living) in Britain for women, who disproportionately occupy the
lower-paid jobs:

"The consequences for so many people and their families are
devastating. Women, as the majority of low-paid workers in this
country, are hit particularly hard. Low pay threatens the great strides
that have been made in gender equality in recent decades because it
undermines women's economic independence. This is a huge loss for
them and for society as a whole."

Again Shinzo Abe offers a vision of a better Japan in which women
have better jobs and improved access to Child Care: Cameron's
platitudes only offer a worse future for Britain's women, as inflation
erodes their already low pay and as the statutory minimum income
per hour is deliberately set to increase by less than the rate of
inflation.

2.9 Concluding comparisons on Shinzo Abe's speech

Finally in the closing Section 7 of his speech, Shinzo Abe quotes
Shimomura again:

"I would like to close my remarks with a different quotation from Dr.
Shimomura, whom I spoke about earlier.This statement can be found

in the preface to his 1960 research paper entitled, "Fundamental Issues in Growth Policies." It is a powerful message from Dr. Shimomura to Japan as it was about to begin its full-scale period of high economic growth.

"It is our own choices and determination and our creative endeavours in the present that will determine our fate ten years from now. What will develop this potential and bring it into realisation is not the unenterprising and passive principle of 'conceding anything to avoid confrontation,' but rather an ambitious and creative robustness. This is a time for us to move forward with confidence, convinced of the creative abilities of the Japanese people."

I believe in the abilities of the Japanese people. The Japanese economy will grow robustly once more through the strength of the Japanese people. Grounded in this belief, I will formulate a Growth Strategy of a nature altogether different from what has come before and execute it resolutely."

Cameron of course, like the previous Conservative leader he most admires, Mrs Thatcher, has no programme at all for improving the lot of the majority of the British people.

3 Concluding Comments on the Abe-Cameron Comparison

Shinzo Abe has a personal philosophy of the inclusion of all the Japanese people in his growth plan, and he is ruling Japan in the interests of all its people. Cameron has no similar philosophy of social and economic inclusiveness and he is ruling the UK in the interests of the already rich and privileged, as his reduction in the tax rate for individuals earning over £150,000 demonstrates.

Cameron offers the UK more of the same failed Thatcherist policies of pointless privatisations, more death to private companies through enabling the seedbed of future British prosperity to be acquired by foreign-based companies funded by the more competent financial-industrial systems in Asia and the EU.

It's all going to work for Japan. Shinzo Abe is very able and focused on doing almost everything necessary to ensure a better future for all the Japanese people. The Japanese Government, led by Shinzo Abe, is a first class government, acting competently to deal with present emergencies, providing the credit-created investment monies to improve Japan's future, and improving the lot of all the Japanese people, while taking no divisive or damaging actions to the current welfare of the Japanese. Shinzo Abe clearly knows what he is doing and where Japan is going.

Cameron has no comparable programme for the improvement of the UK. His cabinet is socially upper class but intellectually defective: a broken government. I do wish Cameron was even minimally competent and not quite so pathetically inadequate by comparison. The Conservative Party under Cameron have turned into a kind of British Republican Party, isolationist and xenophobic, pretty well unelectable except through frightening the electorate by using the idea that any incoming Labour Government might be worse. But the performance of this Cameron-led Coalition Government is so appalling that such a case is very difficult to make.

If the Cameron-led Coalition Government of the UK completely suspended all of its "chase-the-depression-down" economic measures, the economy would actually improve. Instead, failing to deal competently with current emergencies, failing to arrange investment development monies and failing to improve the funding of company investment in the UK, worsening the lot of the British people through an unnecessary fiscal squeeze, and creating great uncertainty and potential division in the UK and the EU - zero out of four – the Coalition has no plan for improvement. The continued existence and activity of the Coalition Government actually worsens the operation of the British economy and the future wealth and welfare of the British people. Things will get better when they are no longer in power. The austerity programme which is the central plank of all their policies was completely unjustified in the past and is totally unnecessary for Britain's future. As Kenneth Kenkichi Kurihara has put it

"If, therefore, greater investment can be financed partly by credits, there is no need for that 'abstinence' which the classical economists

considered necessary for economic progress, any more than there is
for that 'austerity' which some present day underdeveloped countries
impose on already under-consuming populations at the constant peril
of social unrest. Nor is it difficult, in such credit-creating
circumstances, to agree with Keynes' observation that investment and
consumption should be regarded as complementary rather than
competitive."

Kenneth K Kurihara, *Applied Dynamic Economics*, 1963, George
Allen and Unwin, Ltd p60.

4 Conclusions

Shinzo Abe understands Shimomuran economics and he has declared
his intention that Japan will once again practice investment credit
creation on a massive scale to bring about another era of much higher
growth based upon the involvement of all the Japanese people and
their innovative talents especially in the key emerging technologies
in the health sector. He knows exactly what he is doing, he has
considered his policy options in great detail and he is offering
inspiring leadership as well as a detailed programme for the
achievement of his objectives. Japan is fortunate to have such a great
leader in this time of troubles. The Cameron-led Coalition
Government have no idea whatsoever about how to produce a better
future for the British people. They do not understand how wealth
creation works and the positive role that banks can have in a modern
economy. [Britain is very unfortunate to have such an inadequate
leader in this time of troubles.]

The only idea they do practise is to sacrifice national prosperity in
order to achieve fiscal rectitude. They don't understand that such an
approach is completely invalidated by Shimomuran economics, and
they would all be much more at home with the failed policies of the
1930s than in the 21st century. Cameron offers no positive vision of
the future to the British people except for the dismal prospect of
another plateful of Thatcherism and unending rounds of welfare cuts.
His cabinet are equally broken. The people of Britain deserve much
better than this bunch of Eton-led, out-of-touch, callous and inept
clowns.What a painful comparison, between the highly intelligent,

great unifying Japanese Prime Minister Shinzo Abe, acting in the interests of all the Japanese people, and the broken government of the broken Prime Minister Cameron, who has had no experience of a real job, and who fell from Conservative Office into becoming the British Prime Minister without any positive idea about how to lead the British people out of the credit-crunch depression but instead is making things worse for most of the British people."

There is perhaps one major difference between David Cameron and Shinzo Abe. David Cameron wishes to rule Britain for the benefit of his financial backers and their friends, while Shinzo Abe obviously wishes to rule Japan for the benefit of all the Japanese.

4.3 1st July 2013 "The Alternative 2013 Spending Review, Or What Mr Osborne Could Have Said If He Understood Macroeconomics"

This article was originally published on July 1st 2013 at: http://londonprogressivejournal.com/article/view/1537/the-alternative-spending-review-or-what-mr-osborne-could-have-said-if-he-understood-macroeconomics

"The Spending Review by George Osborne delivered on 26 June 2013 had been widely trailed and contained no surprises. It was more of the same - more cuts in the funds of Government departments, more consequential loss of jobs from these cuts, more austerity piled onto the current austerity, more targeted victimisation of the poor and underprivileged, more economic misery inflicted on a depressed economy and on an under-consuming population. Osborne's budget had no significant redeeming features whatsoever. Action to stimulate economic growth was minor while the continuing and deeper cuts were major. The budget for the National Health Service was maintained in real terms but the needs for that service are now much greater than the provision that the real terms budget permits. Meanwhile the move towards the privatisation of the NHS - which Cameron said he would never do - gathers momentum.

More precisely, Cameron said during the last election campaign that the NHS was "Safe in his hands." If challenged now, he might say that privatising the NHS will not damage it. Does anybody believe that?

The Coalition procedure for bringing about the privatisation of the NHS is now clear. It has six stages:

- Deny the NHS sufficient funding to provide the services legally required

- Blame the people running the NHS for consequential service failures

- Use these service failures as a pretext for transferring services piecemeal to the private sector at less cost to the government

- Threaten the existing NHS public service providers with prosecution for service failures so as to limit information about service decline and usefully shut up whistleblowers while pretending to act in the public interest

- Do not require the incoming private service providers to maintain similar service standards to the NHS and do not threaten these new providers with personal criminal prosecution for service failure

- And finally, provide a cheaper and worse service through private health service providers, with better quality and preferred access available only to those who can afford to pay more.

That procedure may be tactically brilliant but seems to me to be close to criminally underhand.

The three-stage procedure for getting Government departments to accept cuts of between 5% and 10% is equally interesting. That process is:

- Ask government departments to consider how they would cope with 15% budget cuts
  - Require lesser cuts of 5% to 10% in the actual announced settlement
  - Ensure the press publication of the cries of gratitude because of the implementation of a lower percentage cut than that threatened.

- That procedure has a close similarity to how some kidnappers treat their hostages. Kidnappers have sometimes threatened their hostages with major injury or even murder and then only inflict minor injury. The hostages are then duly grateful for the reduced damage, not recognising that the kidnappers are entirely responsible for the evil they do and the situation the hostages are experiencing in the first place. The people of Britain and their essential public services are being treated as if they were government hostages, required to be grateful that the damage done by the government is not worse than that initially promised.

But suppose Mr Osborne really understood Shimomuran economics and actually wanted to improve the functioning and performance of the British economy. What could he have said?

- For comparison purposes, here's my version of a constructive speech from a competent chancellor.

****

"The Alternative 2013 Spending Review Speech

"I stand before you today a chastened and humble man, certainly better advised than I was previously, even if I am only a little wiser.

"On the way to the House of Commons this morning I had a Pauline conversion, a vision of a civilised and progressive Britain where all of its children could be free from want, excellently educated, and achieving their full potential within a much more prosperous and fairer society.

"This government now wishes to act in the interests of all the people of Britain. We now propose to take quick action in order to end the mistaken programme of austerity and to stimulate greater private and public investment in the interests of all our people. Given this U-turn in the Government's thinking is so complete, and one of the greatest changes of direction in Britain's history, a brief explanation of the situation in which we now find ourselves is now necessary.

"The Bank of England has, during the last few years, created credit on a massive scale. The total credit created by the Bank of England to support the banks has amounted to about £375 billion - about 25% of the United Kingdom's Gross Domestic Product of about £1.5 trillion. That money, under the most excellent leadership of Mervyn King, was aimed at improving the liquidity of the British banks and has achieved that objective. We did not borrow any money from abroad or from domestic sources to fund that credit creation, so none of that created credit is owed to anyone.

"This Government wishes to acknowledge its great obligation to Mr Mervyn KIng for his wise guidance of the BoE during recent years and hopes he will continue to advise us from another place when he retires from his present position at the end of this month.

"Unfortunately the Bank of England's "Quantitative Easing", which is what they call their credit operations, has done nothing so far to improve the productivity of British industry. The monies provided to the banks have been financial credits, not investment credits. When this Government belatedly realised that more could be done, an additional line of £80 billion of credit was established to improve investment in British industry. Unfortunately the take-up of these investment credits has been very disappointing because we put nothing in place that would ensure their use. The plant machinery in the factories of our SMEs is still generally outdated and requires widespread updating in order to enable effective British competition with the rest of the world. It is a Government objective that this should now be done.

"We have had ma]or recent discussions with the leaders in the Confederation of British Industry, with the TUC and the EEF and with Britain's banks to ensure we can all agree on the need to act together to restore the effectiveness of Britain's economy. All these high contracting parties are fully advised about, and in complete agreement with, these fresh government proposals. We are also very concerned about the need to help the poorest people of Britain and we are holding discussions with several charities to see how best the government can quickly help those in greatest need. We are particularly grateful for the research conducted by the Joseph Rowntree Foundation and their useful recommendations about how best to tackle poverty, and we will be bringing forward proposals during the lifetime of this parliament to assist the achievement of that shared objective.

"Britain must adopt an open conspiracy to make this country great again. There is no shortage of talent in Britain and we wish to place our businesses on an equal footing with those in the best of the rest of the developed world by giving our companies equivalent access to investment credit funding. We really are all in this together. We cannot have a third-rate financial-industrial system which fails to fund our industries because it has no priority to do so. The Government now has such a priority and the banks must comply.

"These new proposals are nothing less than a New Deal for Britain.

This is a New Deal for British industry, which will be able to find the required development capital at their local helpful and co-operative bank, with the banking system willing and able to provide the long term debt necessary to fund greater business liquidity, higher fixed investments and more working capital. A New Deal for the British people, who will be more able to find work in a more rapidly growing economy to pay for all the essential needs, and most of the developing wants, of their families. It is not accidental that we are using the words of President Franklin Delano Roosevelt to describe our activity because his administration, from 1938-44, was the first to act as we are now doing. May our actions be as effective in achieving better economic development as his were.

"The main measures, which will go into effect immediately, are:

"First, with regard to the Bank of England (BoE), new legislation will be passed as soon as possible to define a new mandate for the Bank of England to give the bank the prime purpose of acting to promote the economic growth of the United Kingdom. The BoE will now re-discount a further £150 billion of bank loans to British industry, and that money will be earmarked for use by the recipient banks as long-term investment credit for British-based commerce and industry. These loans will have a term of not less than ten years and an interest rate of 2%, to promote British industrial development.

"Second, an Economic Planning Agency will be set up in Whitehall reporting to the Prime Minister to monitor the effect of these new measures and that Agency will report monthly to the Prime Minster and the Cabinet on economic progress and on any other measures which seem desirable to promote economic growth.

"Third, a financial ombudsman will be created to ensure that British Banks do not turn down useful and commercial business investments as they seem to have done for more than a century. If the existing banks do not wish to become investment credit banks, the government will consider legislation to enable the creation of new local savings banks to collect local savings to fund small and medium sized enterprises, new local authority banks to ensure greater commitment by banks to the community from which their savings originated, and new regional and national investment credit banks to ensure a complete matching coverage of funding institutions with local, regional and national funding needs.

"These new institutions will mirror the more competent SME funding arrangements and other existing industrial funding arrangements in Germany. These new banks will be guaranteed by government, as if fact all banks are in the last resort. There can be no foreign objection to the British Government taking steps to ensure that British domestic industry has access to equivalent financial facilities as these that have existed, and which continue to exist, to fund foreign industry abroad. Given access to equivalent funding sources, we are confident that British innovation and British industry will no longer lose its place in the world and will flourish through the fresh opportunities now made available to it.

"A few numbers will help illustrate the extent of the transformation we plan to bring about. The £150 billion of initial bank loan rediscounting by the Bank of England will, my economists calculate, create a final new level of commercial and industrial funding of about £300 billion because of multiplier effects in the banking system. From our provisional calculations we expect these funds to be initially used to provide an improvement of about £100 billion in business liquidity, about £100 billion in early new plant and equipment investment and about £100 billion in funding higher levels of capital and goods work in progress. It is forecast that if the usual level of tax take of 42% applies to the new investment and to work in progress, government revenue receipts could increase by about £84 billion - an excellent return to government from a better economic understanding and the initial movement of many electrons in the banking system.

Furthermore, that new investment would produce a permanent increase in output of about an extra £100 billion a year, equal to a permanent increase in GDP of about 6.7%, and a permanent rise in government revenue of about £42 billion a year. We think these changes will occur within two years.

"We will be monitoring the final figures for how all this turns out. Some of our economists have argued that, because an extra job in manufacturing industry has historically created another job in the service industries, the final effect will be twice what our initial calculations imply. Others have said that restoration of the economy to a higher growth path will enable the underperforming assets and spare capacity in our industries to respond to the higher levels of demand created by this stimulus, and the final results will be much higher than twice our initial estimates. We think both of these observations have some merit.

"Of one thing we can be certain: the British Government will no longer chase the depression down into a spiral of decline. These measures now proposed, along with other similar measures in the future, will end the long centuries of British economic decline and will place our industries on a higher growth path involving greater prosperity for all our people. Unemployment will fall to a low level. Social security payments will automatically reduce as fuller employment becomes the norm and Government income will cease to be disappointing, ending the need for austerity in government expenditure and all of its ill effects on our people.

"Let the word grow forth at this time, and from this Government, that Britain stands at the beginning of another financial-industrial revolution which will propel our innovative people and our skilled workforce once more into the front rank of world developments.

"We no longer believe that it is appropriate for University student fees to be levied in England and Wales. These proposals will be shelved immediately and the debt obligations to the universities will be honoured. It was never a good idea to make students pay out of their future earnings for higher education, because it inhibits the flowering of the potential of many of our people from poorer backgrounds. Education is one of the main escalators of the gifted. The high wages created by degrees - averaging about an extra 25% throughout the life of an average graduate - place the group of graduates among the highest contributors to the public purse. The main beneficiary from higher education is the Government, which receives higher taxes from the extra earnings of graduates. Investment in education actually offers one of the highest future returns to current expenditure by government. In these circumstances it makes no sense to reduce future government income by discouraging the availability of higher education to all of those who can benefit from it.

"The bedroom tax will be abolished. That tax was causing much more pain than benefit. Housing Associations and local authorities will have access to a new source of investment credit funding to provide low cost housing in our communities and to provide the funds for the construction industry to build new housing to solve the current housing crisis.

"We are aware that new technology in the workplace frequently requires less labour. Sufficiently higher investment, however, often requires more labour and we are interested in seeing that the labour displaced by new technology can be absorbed into industries with higher investment. Ideally the labour displacement effect due to more productive investment in established industries should equal the additional labour demands of new industries. The government will be funding more research into this topic in due course.

"We will ensure the provision of the essential funds for the modernisation of Britain's infrastructure and the protection of its people. The capital monies required by the improvement in precautionary sea defences will be reinstated and will be increased to meet the projected need.

"One item of wage legislation will be enacted. Future wage and salary increases will be divided, with half of the annual percentage increase paid weekly or monthly and the other half paid as a lump sum every 1st November. This measure will limit inflation and provide earners with lump sum funds which research has shown are more likely to be saved, which in turn will increase the emergency funds of families for holidays or to meet unexpected expenses. It will also usefully increase the saving of British families, and in our restructured financial system that will increase bank funds for industry. That measure has proved very effective in Japan, where it may have been another policy initiative originating from the Japanese master economist Osamu Shimomura, and we think it will be as effective in the UK as it was in Japan.

"A few words about the developing international situation are appropriate. The IMF recently recommended that Britain needed to adopt a Plan B because the austerity programme was failing to deliver its stated objectives. This New Deal is our plan B.

"This new policy is completely consistent with the successful examples of higher growth in the economies of the USA from 1938-44, Japan from 1946 to the mid 1970s and China from the mid1970s. We commend this approach to our colleagues in the European Union and the ECB, and to our American and Indian friends, and to all these foreign governments who wish us well. We wish you well also. We hope our example can encourage you to act similarly.

"The ECB has so far created credit of about two trillion Euros to fund the ailing economies of southern Europe. We are all members of the European Union now. These people are part of us. We suggest the ECB should consider, as a matter of the utmost urgency, the provision of new investment credit funds of about 8% of the EU GDP, or about 900 billion Euros to help assist the economic recovery of Europe. These funds would be proportionate to the size of the European economy and the scale of the European need.

"The Japanese Prime Minister, Mr Abe has a parallel programme to ours in Japan. He is, through the Bank of Japan window operations, providing a massive injection of capital - about $1.4 trillion dollars or about 30% of Japan's GDP - via the Japanese financial system into their industrial sector in order to modernise the plant and equipment in Japanese factories. That seems to us to be likely to work. We are not yet quite so brave, but as our programme develops, we will take further and surer steps in the light of our economic progress.

"The major lesson of our modern economic experience is that wealth can be created and destroyed. I do not need to waste any words by telling you how wealth can be destroyed by unwise bank lending - we have all suffered from that. More importantly, no-cost investment credit can be created and supplied as business loans that are repaid out of real increases in output, and these loans create a continuous stream of future wealth through the use of improved plant and machinery and the employment of labour. Investment credit at the

Bank of England on a sufficient scale is the best wealth-creating response to the wealth destruction of the credit crunch. That is the central focus of this spending review.

"Finally I apologise on behalf of this Coalition Government for the unnecessary suffering created by our previously mistaken policies. We know this financial statement is really a mini-budget and is probably too late to affect our fate at the ballot box but we have at least provided an effective recovery platform from which our successors, whatever their political hue, can make further progress."

****

That's my idea of what Osborne could have and should have said. The contrast is painful.

It is very clear that Mr Osborne, like his leader David Cameron, the Prime Minister for the rich, is not up to it. He does not know enough economics, and his mindset is too narrow and too poshly aloof, too smug and self-satisfied for him to be capable of listening to other viewpoints, let alone adopting a more competent and constructive resolution to Britain's current economic problems. Just because the solutions to these long standing problems are beyond him and his advisors does not mean they are beyond everybody. There is a very faint glimmer of hope in the budget in the form of the intention to change the remit of the Bank of England so that it could act to promote economic growth. The Japanese Government did that with the Bank of Japan in 1942, and the French government did something similar under de Gaulle in 1946. But it is a deathbed conversion at the point when most voters would prefer the end of this hopeless Coalition government to any belated "jam tomorrow" conversion.

The recent document about the need for infrastructure investment (see "Investing in Britain's Future" at https://www.gov.uk/ government/uploads/system/uploads/attachment_data/file/209279/ PU1524_IUK_new_template.pdf) seems to be more of a political plea for a second term in office for this failed Coalition government than demonstrating any urgency or any marked desire for the higher economic growth which would invalidate the need for the current Coalition government's austerity programme. "Investing in Britain's Future" could be usefully re-titled "What we could have done, but didn't do, but we might do after 2016", and resembles an epitaph for a failed government more than a practical prescription for future action. Above all, that new document illustrates the appalling fact that this Coalition Government came to power in Britain without any constructive idea in their heads about how better to govern Britain. Their Thatcherism Phase Two, 1930s policy, will not do, and is entirely inappropriate to modern Britain. It was never going to work and it has taken them over three miserable years for the Government to realise that, with more misery and pain promised as long as they are in office.

When Japan wanted to learn how to grow rapidly, they sent their businessmen and economists to America in late 1945 and early 1946, to find out how the Americans had produced their economic miracle and to replicate it in Japan under the slogan "Western Technology, Japanese Spirit." Which they did. When the Chinese wanted to learn how to grow rapidly, they sent investigating economists, businessmen and political leaders to Japan in the mid 1970s to find out how to copy Japan's growth-accelerating formula and to discover how to transform China into a prosperous modern economy. Which they did.

The eighth paragraph of the G8 Final Communique, From Lough Erne 2013, said that

"Our urgent priority is to promote growth and jobs, particularly for the young and long-term unemployed. We will continue to nurture the global recovery by supporting demand, securing our public finances and reforming our economies to deliver growth.."

There was nothing in Osborne's financial statement which addressed that urgent priority to promote growth and jobs, particularly for the young and long-term unemployed. Nor do any of his actions support demand, secure higher public finances or reform the UK economy to promote growth. Quite the contrary - nil out of four.

An incoming Labour Government could certainly turn Britain's fortunes around if they so choose. The team of Miliband and Balls are going to have a greater opportunity to remake Britain than has existed since the reforming Labour Government of 1945.

It is now too late, much too late, for this "dog of a (Conservative-led Coalition) Government" to mend its ways. They are going to stay as they are, economically inept and monstrously complacent, until they are booted out of office. If they had not passed the bill awarding themselves a five year term that would probably have happened already. It is more than half-time in their five year term. The only thing that keeps them in power is their legally created capacity to cling to it.

The contrast between what a British Chancellor could say if he was adequately informed and sufficiently intelligent, with the stumbling bumbling of this uneducated fool is almost too great to be bearable. Judging him by results - and if you judge people by their results, you will never do them wrong - Osborne, whether you call him George or Gideon or Jeffrey, is by far the worst Chancellor Britain may ever have had. As Keynes said in the 1930s:

"It is not an accident that it is a Conservative Government that have got us in this mess. It is the natural result of their philosophy."

Of course it is. Osborne is trying to apply the Conservative "solutions" of the 1930s to the problems of the 2010s. These so-called "solutions" - wage cuts, the shrinkage of government activity, the attack on people's living standards, the high unemployment and social misery inevitably resulting from these mistaken policies - did not work then. They are no more likely to work now.

What a shame! What a lost opportunity!

What an idiot!"

****

At location 4461 of 6953 of Lord Robert Skidelsky's Kindle book *"Britain since 1900 - a Success Story?"* Margaret Thatcher is reported as having said that

' "The real case against socialism," she said in 1977, "is not its economic efficiency. Much more fundamental is its immorality." '

With the experience of a third of a century of neoclassical Thatcherism it is now obvious that the real case against neoclassical macroeconomics is its economic inefficiency, because it fails to provide the funds to convert personal invention into factory-floor innovation, with the local loss of income to the inventor, income to the innovator, and jobs to the locality as well as the complete loss of various taxes arising from increases in national income to the Government. And much more fundamental is the callous immorality of neoclassical economics which cuts jobs and welfare without providing any remedy to these losses in work and welfare income.

Much better policies are possible, as the next section illustrates.

4.4 28 April 2015 "An Anti-Austerity 2015 UK Budget"

This article was originally published on April 28th 2015 at: https://medium.com/@georgetaitedwards/an-anti-austerity-2015-uk-budget-fd9ccb1b552a

"1 Introduction

Suppose that the United Kingdom

- Elected an Anti-Austerity Alliance Coalition on 7 May 2015 and
- That Coalition practised Shimomuran-Wernerian no-cost investment credit creation economics

What might its first budget look like?

2 Purpose

The purpose of this article is to calculate some of the government budget effects of the implementation of some of the measures suggested in the nine articles coauthored with Bryan Gould which set out an anti-austerity agenda at http://londonprogressivejournal.com/user/view/6214.

3 Four Selected Key Measures

This article illustrates some of the budgetary effects of implementing the following major measures:

3.1 Reversing the £20bn austerity cuts
3.2 Transferring an additional £20bn pa to the NHS
3.3 Reducing English University student fees to zero through a £30bn plus annual transfer to fund free university education for English, Welsh and NI students as well as for EU nationals resident or seeking an education in the rUK
3.4 Creating Bank of England (BoE) investment credit of £75bn a year for long-term low-cost SME loans.

4 A No-Cost Budget for British Economic Recovery The Coalition Government have produced an economic disaster and a downturn in Britain's fortunes equivalent to the destruction caused by a small war. These policies have no possible future. See https://medium.com/@georgetaitedwards/osborne-s-dream-of-the-continuation-of-neoclassical-economics-is-a-boot-stamping-on-human-face-c3d0b97a94f4 The alternative proposals set out in paras 3.1 to 3.4 above are the incomplete starting point for a much better future for the British people.

The source of funding for each of these measures and their effect on the Government budget is calculated in the sections below, and briefly discussed in the following four sections and explained in section 5. The first three items are no-cost consumer or consumption creation ("deficit funding without the borrowing") items while the fourth item is growth-creating BoE no-cost investment credit creation earmarked for final use by UK SMEs.

4.1 Reversing the £20 bn a year austerity cuts These social funds can be completely provided by credit creation of £20bn pa at the BoE for four years. There would be neither borrowing nor cost in that provision for the Government, although if one wished to follow established Tokyo Consensus conventions, the BoE could write down "savings of the people" and take out a loan counterparted against itself. Alternatively it could write down "Treasury Request" as it did when it created £375bn of credit to finance Clearing Bank survival. In either case, it should write off this theoretical "charge" it owes to itself through that consumer credit creation, as China usually does. (See https://medium.com/@georgetaitedwards/the-public-debt-of-japan-and-china-e82292595d7a The Public Bank of China creates loans to fulfil government and growth objectives, and the Chinese Government does not record all, and often writes off many, "non-performing loans". Since there is no intention of UK Government repayment of these funds, they should be immediately written off.) The need for the unemployment and income support aspects of these social fund transfers would reduce as the economy blossomed but new needs might be created, for example, by the pensions required by an ageing population. The average tax take in the UK is usually about 42% but the realistic revenue funds arising from the restoration of support provision would probably result in much less than that, because much of the extra income of the poor and disadvantaged would be used to buy food and other zero-rated essentials (such as children's clothes and shoes) on which no tax is raised, so I have assumed a low 21% tax take.

If an additional £40bn of benefit lost in 2013–14 and 2014–15 is also paid in 2015/16—as in my opinion it should be, to restore the previous status quo of the poor and underprivileged in our society—then the government might receive, on my estimates, £12.6bn of additional revenue in 2015/16 and £4.2bn a year from benefit restoration thereafter. Not a bad return for no cost whatsoever.

4.2 Transferring an additional £20bn pa to the NHS Similarly an appropriate injection of NHS funding amounting to £20bn a year should be created and maintained. That would produce through the usual 42% tax take, an extra £8.4 bn each year at no cost to Government revenues.

4.3 Reducing English University student fees to zero through a £30bn plus annual transfer to fund university education Persons resident in England, Northern Ireland and Wales deserve the same free access to higher education as the Scots or as (say) the Germans. A no-cost £30bn transfer is likely to add about £12.6bn to Government revenues at no cost through taxation on the expenditure of the funds released by this change.

4.4 Creating BoE investment credit of £75bn a year for long-term low-cost SME loans This is the major investment credit creation proposed in this article. The proposal is that the BoE should create £75bn a year of investment credit, earmarked for final use as long-term lending to SMEs at local level via a cooperative banking system. The provision of local banks committed to the success of local industry is a prerequisite for this activity. See para 3.2 of https://medium.com/@georgetaitedwards/how-to-create-an-economic-miracle-d2ffa95e6c73.

5 The costs and benefits of these anti-austerity measures The cost of all of the above measures is zero and the gains to British prosperity through economic growth are substantial. A large part of that gain is the revenue benefits which accrue to the British Government through the expenditure of the above indicated funds. The pre-June 2015 Coalition Government does not, of course, understand the process of wealth creation at all, and their only focus has been on the side-issue of making economies in the budgeted cost of government. Their obsession with the objective of achieving a balanced budget blinds them to the fact that there is a much better way to govern Britain—a way that increases the wealth and welfare of all, as proposed here.

5.1 Estimated Increased Budgets For a 2015 UK Government from Credit Creation

The restoration of all benefits at £20bn a year, assuming 21% (half of usual average UK tax take of 42%) gives government income from this source of £4.2bn, and the one-of payment of benefits lost in the two previous gives rise to a total of c£40bn, which might produce a tax income of 8.4bn.

The transfers of £20bn NHS funds plus the£30bn funding of university fees in England, Wales and NI would produce extra £21bn total tax receipts. Taking both the above together, these items would add about £33.6bn to government income in 2015/16 and £25.2bn in subsequent years.

The £75 billion a year of new investment credit creation provided by the Bank of England ("Window Guidance" rediscounting long-term SME loans, just as the Bank of Japan did from 1945 to 1974). [Note that this initial investment credit creation of credit is at the level of about 5% of GDP, that is at about half the £150 bn a year proposed in Part 5 of the nine articles co-authored with Bryan Gould—see http://londonprogressivejournal.com/article/view/2127/economic-policies-for-an-incoming-labour-government-part-of —because this article deals only with providing growth funds for SMEs and not for the other half of UK industrial and commercial companies.] I have assumed the additional annual SME funding would be used as £25bn additional liquidity, £25bn for raw materials and WIP, and £25bn for new fixed plant and equipment investment. So SME money in the bank would increase by £25bn and there would be an extra £50bn of expenditure.
Assuming a multiplier of 2, the SME expenditure stimulation of £50bn might create another £50bn of demand.. Government income from all that would be £42bn—the average tax take of 42% of £100bn. Assuming a capital output ratio of about four, there would be a permanent increase in real output of about an extra £12.5 bn a year. Assuming BoE loans were provided to the secondary banks at an interest rate of 2%, there would be an line of interest payments increasing at £1.5bn a year.
The total effect on Government revenues from these activities would lie between £77bn in 2015/16 and £73bn in 2018/19. The UK Government current account deficit of c£80bn would be reduced by

over 90% by these policies, and possibly completely reversed because these assumptions are all on the low side (and no allowance has been made welfare cost reductions due to increased prosperity).

As Bryan Gould and I say in section 3.8 above:
"The experience of other countries shows that investment credit economics works by creating wealth in the productive sector of the economy. The loans made are almost completely repaid (the failure rate is typically about 2.5%) out of the growth of the economy resulting from the additional investment. The failure rate of these loans matters little in any case because the loans cost nothing to create; their consequences matter, however, because they produce their targeted effect in reducing poverty, stabilising the banking system, and creating widespread prosperity through many flourishing private industries in all the areas of the country."
And
"Unemployment will fall to a low level. Social security payments will automatically reduce as fuller employment becomes the norm and Government income will cease to be disappointing, ending the need for austerity in government expenditure and bringing to an end all of its ill effects for our people. "

The effect on UK GDP— adding the additional consumer demand, investment and WIP, multiplier effects and real growth together, indicates an annual growth in the UK economy of about 8% a year. The practice of the Tokyo Consensus Simomuran-Wernerian economics in the UK leads to an estimated growth rate similar to that of the China Sea economies, as might be expected. From 1945 to 1952 Japan zoomed from war devastation beyond its highest level of pre-war prosperity, at an average growth rate of 10.2%, using precisely these techniques. See https://medium.com/@georgetaitedwards/how-japan-zoomed-from-war-devastation-into-prosperity-1945-52-92cad27eea81 The no-cost creation of investment credit is the secret of the high economic growth of China, South Korea and Taiwan. EU leaders and others please note this illustration of the credit creation system.

6 Conclusions

6.1 The Importance of adequate SME funding All large enterprises started as small SMEs and grew to greatness through effective funding mechanisms. The savings made available for investment by SMEs—the domestic and foreign funds which could be used for productive investment—are woefully inadequate to enable to enable the full flowering of local SME invention. This is valid not just for the UK but everywhere in the Anglosphere and even in Germany. Only investment credit creation can produce an economic explosion by funding the conversion of nearly all local individual invention via a local entrepreneur into factory floor production.

The most cursory look at highly developed final products confirms the role of SMEs in their production. A Boeing 747 has over five million parts, over half of them fasteners—screws, bolts, rivets, glues—and the vast majority of these parts are made by specialist SME producers. Werner von Braun used to say of the Apollo 11 rockets "There it goes—over 100,000 moving parts—all of them provided by the lowest bidder—and it all works!" Of course he did not repeat that remark after the Challenger disaster.

The Japanese car industry in the UK is not a net advantage to the British economy because these car plants are assembly factories for imported Japanese car parts. All of the company and car components —the initial capital, the automated production machinery, the metal sheets, the paints, wires, windows, electrical items and engines—are sourced from Japan. Local labour is the only item in the production process. Britain needs a domestically-owned car industry which buys the local SME outputs as part of its future economy. It needs to focus on domestic high value products which its highly educated workforce could provide, given an equal chance.

6.2 Shimomuran-Wernerian Economics This essay is a worked example of the application of the observations in "How to create an economic miracle in the UK or elsewhere" which is at Appendix 1 and https://medium.com/@georgetaitedwards/how-to-create-an-economic-miracle-d2ffa95e6c73.
The current vogue for sadistic neoclassical macroeconomics cannot prevail because it offers no hope and no adequate development rate for the Anglosphere economies. The mistaken economic beliefs of

neo-classical economics needs to be replaced by the mindset of Shimomuran-Wernerian economics.

6.3 BoE credit creation is not new There is nothing new about the creation of credit by the Bank of England, for £375 bn of credit creation was used to stabilise the liquidity and preserve the operation of five British Clearing Banks and £80 bn of such credit was created to support Vince Cable's incomplete proposal to extend business loans to industry. Previous attempts to improve the investment funding of SMEs have foundered on Clearing Bank opposition to any changes to improve the existing situation. The current concentration of 84% of UK bank savings in six banks, which drain local UK savings but provide no taps or local investment is largely responsible for current failings. There are about 5 million SMEs in the UK which receive virtually no support from the branches of the UK banking system except for the standard retail service of a money transfer system. Germany has seven regional banks, 431 Sparkassen (or local savings banks) and a network of 15,600 branches to provide SME loans from German savings. Each Sparkassen—all 431 of then— concentrate on providing business loans to SMEs in the area where it is located, and each has an interest in, and commitment to, ensuring the economic success of its native village, city or region.
Britain has nothing remotely similar and needs such a system. Bank reform as set out in part 8 and improvements in the machinery of government as set out in part 9 of the Gould-Edwards articles are essential handmaidens to improve British economic development. The fresh aspect of the calculations in this article is the use of BoE credit creation for positive social purposes to improve living standards, prosperity and economic growth, and not just use it use as a financial crutch for an inadequate banking system.
6.4 The control of inflation The underlying rate of inflation will not be much affected by these measures. At most an extra 1% pa might possibly arise, but inflation does not occur when the goods in demand (eg foodstuffs and clothing) are available in plenty in the supermarkets and shops of a nation and when adequate spare capacity due to higher investment makes the provision of goods more profitable and price increases more risky. Additions to credit in the banking system by SMEs and wage and salary earners do not give

rise to additional inflation, as Shimomura has remarked in the work which earned him his doctorate.

6.5 Shimomuran-Wernerian economics rebalances the economy
One major advantage of these proposals is to give financial help to the poor and underprivileged, and investment help to the millions of SMEs in the regions of the United Kingdom. Collapsing Anglosphere economies tend to shrink back into what some have described as "capital cities masquerading as national states" as centrally-based politicians maintained major investments in the capital and its surroundings but neglected required investments in the country's regions. This is as obvious in Russia and it is in the UK. The practice of this fresh-to-the-Anglosphere economics improves the lot of the poor and the regions and once again enables the roots of invention to scale up into innovation in all the towns and villages of a country. There is no other available economic option which does that. There is no need for a revolution in income distribution, for this economics permits the rich to keep their wealth while enabling a widespread, broadly based economic recovery of the previously declining industrial areas of a nation.

6.7 A partial illustration This article does not cover most of the bases mentioned in the more wide-ranging nine articles co-authored with Bryan Gould but it does provide a basic budget demonstrating how four of the major factors might affect the British Budget from 2016 to 2019. Of course much more should and could be done as argued elsewhere.

7 Overarching Conclusion An anti-austerity UK budget could reverse much of the Coalition damage done to family incomes and SME prospects and could set Britain on a path to continuing future prosperity with a widely distributed locally based economic recovery. The numbers indicate that even the limited measures quoted above solve the deficit problem within a year, restore social fairness and help the quality of the NHS, as well as setting the UK on a higher trend of economic growth. For further information see http://www.gresham.ac.uk/lectures-and-events/lessons-we-can-learn-from-the-success-of-the-japanese-growth-system and see http://www.gresham.ac.uk/lectures-and-events/the-curious-case-of-the-economist-the-west-forgot-the-life-and-times-of-dr-osamu and https://medium.com/@georgetaitedwards/the-rough-guide-to-shimomuran-economics-e9dca42c6808 [That lecture is reproduced in full in Section 4.9 below.]

The malign prescriptions of neoclassical economics and its continual depression-producing results cannot continue forever. Shimomuran-Wernerian macroeconomics is the best available path to prosperity once the politicians of the West understand the effectiveness of that option, as this article illustrates."

4.5 The Absence of Economic Alternatives to Neo-Classical Economics in British and Western Universities and the comparison of the Washington, Berlin and Tokyo Consensus Zones

The greatest living economist - Professor Richard Andreas Werner - began his seminal book, "*new Paradigm in Macroeconomics - Solving the Riddle of Japanese Macroeconomic Performance*" by listing in five pages the complete and unfortunate victory of a minor political macroeconomics - neoclassical economics - in the political life, universities, media and business thinking in the West.

As Professor Werner points out, it is nearly impossible to learn any alternative macroeconomics in almost any Western university because [in 2005, and little has changed since then] nothing but neoclassical economics is taught. No graduation in any other form of economics can be had, because no employer (in business, the media or the universities themselves) would accept any other form of economics education.

Many individual and academic economists do have alternative views to the malign dominance of neoclassical economics but the universities in which they are employed do not offer any alternative economics with the result that there is no collective alternative macroeconomic viewpoint.

There are three major economic systems in the world. These are:

1) The Washington Consensus

2) The Berlin Consensus

3) The Tokyo Consensus

There are also two major traditions in economic thinking. The first of these is the top down theoretical tradition which states assumptions and builds logical and mathematical models upon these - that's the Washington neoclassical consensus "castle in the air" which dominates media discussion and political action in the West. The alternative is the realistic German Historical School which builds upon observation and argues an economics constructed from the bottom up - that's how the Berlin and Tokyo consensus macroeconomics operate.

The following article which explains the difference between these zones was originally published on 26th June 2014 at: https://medium.com/@georgetaitedwards/a-comparison-of-the-washington-berlin-and-tokyo-consensus-zones-221e7e53018b and on 10th August 2014 at http://londonprogressivejournal.com/article/view/1894/comparison-of-the-washington-berlin-and-tokyo-consensus-zones-which-one-really-works

26 June 2014 "A Comparison of the Washington, Berlin, and Tokyo Consensus Zones

-Which one really works?

1 Introduction

There are three major alternative sets of economic understanding in the world, each operating a different system of an economic consensus. Each zone assumes it has all the answers to the most effective operation of the economies in its zone, and they cannot all be right. These three zones are:

- The Washington Consensus Zone, where a neo-classical restrictive monetarism reigns supreme, supported by the United States and its major allies, and policed and recommended by various "international" American-based and US-dominated organisations (such as the IMF, the OECD, the "World Bank", etc)

- The Berlin Consensus, operating in and dominating the Eurozone, where Germany reigns supreme through the national and local banking commitment to industrial development, and especially through the commitment of its 135 Sparkassen banks with their 12,600 branches to the 2.148 million SMEs ("mittelstand") in Germany, and

- The Tokyo Consensus Zone, comprising the main four nations of the China Sea economies (China, Japan, South Korea and Taiwan) where Shimomuran economics is the ascendant economic understanding and is fully and effectively practised with minor variations.

2 Major Attributes of Each Zone

Each zone is characterised by

- a dominant economic philosophy

- an economic structure, or recipe for presumed success, promoted by the dominant national government or governments within each zone (except in the special case of Germany in the EU)

- an observed set of economic outcomes, and

- a different set of future potentials for economic growth and human development.

2.1 The Washington Consensus Zone

The dominant economic philosophy throughout the Washington Consensus Zone is neo-classical economics, with its emphasis on private enterprise solutions regardless of the economic circumstances of any nation or the social and economic history of its people.

The associated economic structure involves

- governments which have borrowed heavily on the international financial markets, originally to fund tax cuts for the relatively rich and ultimately to provide a pretext for the now-widespread policies of austerity and budget cuts

- an independent central bank, with an emphasis on restricting credit creation with the stated aim of achieving low inflation

- partly, fully or increasingly privatised national facilities, such as health, education, transport and communication systems

Leading inexorably to the economic outcomes of

- the shifting of national income from the majority of its population in favour of domestic corporate profits and international interest payments to the already rich and privileged

- the sale of large domestic industries to foreign buyers and the associated national economic weakening through future dividends being sent abroad

- the increasing collapse of SMEs within the nations practising the Washington Consensus due to the lack of supportive local banks

- the long-term decline in the living standards of most families through higher unemployment, lower social contract facilities (lower social security funds and unemployment and poorer access to higher cost health facilities, education, etc) and the increasing impoverishment of the already poor.

All of these outcomes are already obvious in the major nations practising the Washington Consensus (such as the USA and the UK) and in virtually all of these less developed nations obliged to adopt the Washington Consensus solutions as a condition for receiving international aid.

The international organisations attempting to enforce the Washington Consensus on its client states produce relatively worthless reports because they do not pay any attention whatsoever to local conditions. The OECD reports, for example, recommend the usual litany of neo-classical economics solutions because the visiting teams do not need to even look out of the window to tailor their report to the specific national circumstances of the nation on which they will report. They do of course mention where they are but when it comes to recommendations, they assume they already know all the answers— one neoclassical remedy with all its ramifications is suggested as a solution which will fit the needs and circumstances of all countries.

Except it doesn't. The industrial decline of the USA and the UK and the increasing impoverishment of their people should have made even the most blinkered of the neoclassicists look up.

Neoclassical economics is fulfilling the dire predictions of Marxism. There are better solutions than running the economy mainly for the benefit of the already rich and international capital, which is what neo-classical economics obviously brings about. It is not triumphing, it is not useful, it is not beautiful, it has been rejected in the major country in the Eurozone and in the Tokyo Consensus zone, which both have the possibility of a greater innovative capability and the production of a more widespread prosperity and a more full human development than the Washington Consensus is likely to provide. Even the rich have not voted for what is happening—it is not in their long-term interest that the West loses much of the world.

2.2 The Berlin Consensus Zone

United Europe is dominated by the economic success of United Germany, which success partly rests upon the 135 Sparkassen or local savings banks which are each committed through their 12,600 branches to the local success of the 2.148 million Small and Medium sized enterprises (SMEs) of Germany. About 80% of German savings are available to these local SMEs for local investment purposes. Larger German companies (AG & GmbH) have a Supervisory Board (Aufsichtsrat) which appoints the Management Board (Vorstand), and the executives of major German banks are invariably on the Aufsichtsrat of several major companies where these bankers facilitate the funding of the investment plans for the generally larger industrial companies they advise.

The dominant economic philosophy of Germany is industrial banking. For more information on that tradition, see

http://londonprogressivejournal.com/article/view/1512/nations-get-what-their-financialindustrial-systems-deliver-a-comparative-analysis-of-three-different-groups-of-financialindustrial-systems

The industrial banking tradition, with the commitment of domestic bankers to national success through the provision of long-term loans from banks to private companies, has until recent years dominated the post-war growth in Western Europe and has culminated in the formation of United Europe and the Eurozone. However the relative economic success of Germany and the dominance of German industry has led to the institutions of the European Union being dominated by Germany and German politicians. What should have happened after the credit crunch was the adoption of the Sparkassen tradition and structure throughout all of the states of United Europe to enable the more full flowering of the millions of local EU SMEs. Instead German dominance has led to the use of financial credit creation by the ECB to support a Washington Consensus solution for the weaker industrial economies of the EU. That activity has reduced the prosperity of the EU people, led to a backlash against the EU institutions, and dimmed the future prospects of the EU.

The European Union was not designed to be operated as if it were a German Empire. The economically weaker states of Europe are not in the EU to be exploited by the strongest state—that has never been the basis of the European Union, which was designed as a co-operative venture for the benefit of all of the people of the nations involved.

The response to the recent crisis should not be the abandonment of the industrial banking tradition by the weaker European states but the reinforcement of that tradition by the ECB. This could be done through ECB investment credit creation (at the rate of about 8% to 10% of EU GDP) being funnelled through as earmarked investment credit funding to all the local banks in the EU for use by local SMES in all of the villages and mini-economies within the EU, and by larger industries. The successful German economic model should be replicated at every level in the EU, as it is in Germany, to encourage a swift recovery from the credit crunch. That would work to re-establish and re-provide the prosperity recently removed.

The example of the EU motor vehicle industry illustrates the predominant success of German industry. There are a dozen domestically owned vehicle mass production companies (each receiving local and regional capital loans from supportive banks) in Germany which directly employed 886,000 people in 2005, with each company supported in turn by domestic steel-producing plants and clusters of SMEs providing specialist vehicle-parts, in all manufacturing a total of about 5.7 million vehicles in 2013. At the other end of the scale, Britain has no domestically owned mass production car companies and the British-based foreign companies which do produce motor vehicles in the UK are importing funds for investment and car parts from their home economy to produce their final products, resulting in a net cost to the British balance of payments.

The beautiful local subcultures of United Europe hold a vast potential for the more full development of much of the potential of mankind. The current impoverishment of the people of many of the Southern states of the EU could result in the dissolution of the EU if the better solution (as proposed above) is not adopted. If the partly competent administration led by Angela Merkel does not wish to preside over the dissolution of the EU, then she and her administration need to take early and effective action to ensure EU-wide recovery and prosperity soon, or the newly resurgent

electoral nationalism in the disaffected nations of the EU is likely to
cause that ever-greater union to fail in fulfilling its great promise to
all concerned and to dissolve in a resurgence of negative nationalism.

2.3 The Tokyo Consensus Zone

The dominant economic philosophy of the Tokyo Consensus zone is
Shimomuran economics. The key aspects of that economic policy
are:

- the deliberate economic management of the country by an
intelligent government with the objective of achieving explicit
national objectives

- the provision of large flows (typically 10% to 20% of GDP) of
no-cost investment credit creation by the Central Bank to fund
productive investments of up to date, modern plant and machinery in
all of the manufacturing and service industries and in the SMEs of
the economy

- the monitoring and continual management of the economy through
well-informed government action based on Economic Planning
Agency advice and the continual adjustment of policy to achieve
altering goals

- the adherence of government economic policy to Shimomuran
principles, which are

- the creation of credit principally for productive industrial and
commercial enterprise

- the policy setting of the interest rate equal to the best estimate of
  the inflation rate in factory gate prices (so that money becomes a
  counterpart of real resources)

- the creation of an economy of abundant capital at all levels and for
  all industries in the economy, and

- legislation for the payment of wage and salary increases as about
  half in weekly wages or monthly salaries, and the rest in an annual
  bonus: this policy limits inflation and encourages the saving of
  part of lump-sum bonuses, and alters the pattern of demand to
  increase the affordability of expensive items, as well as improving
  the security of households through their higher access to personal

savings- the creation of a rational bank savings structure, in which time savings are inflation proofed through higher interest rates and immediately available monies slightly lose their value

- the management of growth and inflation through a combination of measures which have a demonstrated track record of success.

These aspects are not an exhaustive list but are only the main common features of the major nations of the Tokyo Consensus Zone (China, Japan, South Korea and Taiwan) although they each have local variants as changing and different national circumstances continually reshape economic policy. The machinery of government for the achievement of these aims, as well as the extent of reporting of these, also varies according to national objectives and local circumstances (eg the extent of credit creation by the BoJ is almost fully measured in Japan, while the apparently same Chinese data has numerous stated exclusions, such as the exclusion of non-performing loans or the rediscount limits allowed for in provincial People's Bank of China bank branches, etc).

A few paragraphs about two of the major countries of the Tokyo Consensus zone (on China and Japan) seems appropriate, as well as similarly framed comments on the first major nation which put into practise the embryo of what has now emerged as the Tokyo Consensus—the USA from 1938 to 1944.

2.3.1 China

After the 29 September 1972 Nixon-inspired rapprochement between China and Japan (which signalled the formal end of WW2 hostilities between these countries) the Chinese negotiating delegations reported back to the Chinese Communist Party leaders the observed immense and obvious degree of Japanese economic development in 1972. Unlike any Western nation, the Chinese government resolved to understand the theory and practice of the economic understanding which had propelled Japan, in less than three decades, from being a war-devastated economy in 1945 to one of the world's major industrial powers, and numerous Chinese delegations were sent to Japan to investigate, understand and report upon how best China could replicate the Japanese growth-accelerating processes.

The extent of Chinese economic understanding can perhaps best be illustrated by the observation that in a Chinese book about major world economists, Dr Osamu Shimomura is listed as Japan's most important postwar economist. That source of course only repeats what the Japanese assert, but I have yet to see such an acknowledgement or recognition in any of the economic textbooks used as teaching materials in Western universities.

Nearly all of the leading western nations (the USA, where ICC originated; the UK, where many of its universities are perhaps first class in almost everything except macroeconomics; nearly all of the EU nations, where there is no lack of realistic economic analysis skills; Russia, currently creating investment credits for the Moscow zone but apparently ignoring the needs of much of the rest of the country; the economists of the four natural resource-rich giants of Australia, Brazil, Canada and again Russia; and many others) could have done as China did. They could have investigated the causes of the Japanese economic miracle and copied the transferable economic technology back home. But they didn't. Britain's NEDO very nearly did, producing a 1980 document entitled "Transferable Factors in Japan's Economic Success." That paper was stamped as "Confidential" and not placed in the public domain and was ignored by the Thatcher government. A banker who was involved in the production of that report once told me that the UK Clearing Banks had nothing to do with that Report's security classification, but I doubt that.

Whatever one thinks about the Chinese Communist Party, its recent leaders during the last half century have been formidably intelligent. The same description cannot be applied to some recent Western leaders who have been much less well advised about economic issues. The Chinese government has pursued a policy of using no-cost investment credit to develop every aspect of the Chinese economy, and in every province of China. Although the coastal zone Chinese provinces have grown more rapidly than those in the central and the western zones, the Government has continually implemented various measures to ensure more even development and more widespread Chinese prosperity. One principal initiative has been the implementation of the "Chinese Dream" of the construction of 400 new cities (each sized at about one million people) during the

2000-2020 period, as well as the updating of all existing Chinese cities, with the parallel relocation of large branches of much of Chinese industry to more western and highland provinces. Chinese living standards are increasing quickly for all classes in China.

The Chinese Government has put into place all the machineries of growth which existed in high-growth Japan, with the result that China has become the major potential hegemonic challenger to the USA during the next couple of decades. After the Chinese teams had completed their 1970s investigations of Japanese growth policies and procedures, and advised the Japanese Government what they had learned, the Japanese foreign ministry on 31 August 1980 released a press statement that "China will emerge as a tremendous economic and military power in the 21st century," as is happening.

2.3.2 Japan

After the end of the Second World War, Japan appeared to be in an impossible economic position. Several Western economists produced reports predicting a dismal future for the Japanese people, painting the picture of an overcrowded Asian island with inadequate raw materials and insufficient arable land adequately to feed its population. The American occupation authorities required the Japanese Government to practice a balanced budget, so the Keynesian route to higher demand and consumption was theoretically not available to that Government—it could not borrow its way out of the post-war depression. So it created credit without any borrowing either domestically or abroad.

What the post-war Japanese governments did was practice Shimomuran economics. The BoJ, which had been given the objective of facilitating economic growth since 1942, from 1945 provided gigantic flows of no-cost investment credit creation (none of it depending on foreign borrowing) initially to restore the essential infrastructure of Japan. The arteries of the economy—Japanese roads and communication facilities—and the essential facilities for population survival—new housing and food supply and distribution facilities, schools, hospitals and civic buildings—were targeted for the receipt of capital investment during the immediate post war period. This caused relatively high inflation but was a vital first stage of the economic recovery of the nation. Part of Dr Osamu

Shimomura's disagreement with Bank of Japan officials [who argued in the 1950s and 1960s that the control of inflation was more important than economic development] may have originated from that post war experience, because he knew from experience that economic development was far more important than inflation.

Foreign observers, visiting Japan in the late 1940s, seeing the great extent of Japanese economic recovery, sometimes stated that the war damage done in Japan must have been much less than that previously estimated. But the pictures of Tokyo immediately after the war—the cityscape of ruined buildings, and all the evidence of the total destructiveness of the Curtis Lemay Tokyo firebombing, which on just one night—on 9/10 March 1945—destroyed 15.8 square miles of Tokyo, killing hundreds of thousands of Japanese workers, illustrates the immense extent of the damage. As the historian Gabriel Kolko has remarked in his 1968 book

"The Operation Meetinghouse firebombing of Tokyo on the night of 9/10 March 1945 was the single deadliest air raid of World War II; greater than Dresden, Hiroshima, or Nagasaki as single events."

See Kolko, Gabriel (1990) [1968]. The Politics of War: The World and United States Foreign Policy, 1943–1945. pp. 539–40.

The Government of Japan from 1949-50 provided—via the BoJ investment credit creation—funds for transmission through Japan's banking system to productive investments in SMEs and to major industries, partly to fund increases in liquidity and working capital but mainly focused on providing up- to-date plant and machinery in all of the manufacturing and service industries and in the SMEs in the economy. These Governments continually monitored and managed the progress of the economy through the information provided by Japan's EPA and by continually adjusting policy to achieve their changing goals.

A vast amount of information about the economic progress of Japanese trade and industry and the structure of its development is provided in the Economic Planning Agency's *Economic Survey Of Japan* (published annually by the Japan Times since 1945). These documents provide the vast wealth of information—better quality information, so far, than that produced by any other major economy —about the progress of every aspect of the Japanese economy.

The Japanese intention in using Shimomuran Investment Credit Economics appears to have been, and still seems to be, very narrowly focused—like Dr O Shimomura himself, they only seem to want to create a trading advantage for Japan, in order to be able to afford to buy from abroad the key raw materials and resources required to feed and productively employ all their people.

Shinzo Abe has reintroduced Shimomuran economics and a "Japan of abundant capital" in his recent policy statement and in his government's activities following on from the failure of the attempted adoption of Washington Consensus policies by the Bank Japan during the last decade of the 20th century and the first decade of the 21st. See Professor Richard Werner's book "Princes of the Yen" where these events are fully documented. If anyone wishes to compare and contrast the experience of a major nation practising Shimomuran high-growth economies for several decades followed by Washington Consensus policies for almost two decades then Japan is an interesting illustration of the results of these different policies.

The role of Dr Osamu Shimomura (1910-89) in the success of Japan is partly hidden by the absence of his works, and the absence of an accurate translation of any of his works, in the West. We know that Dr Shimomura produced a paper on the Japanese multiplier which earned him his doctorate, that he was directly responsible for the management of prices and that he had views about how to manage wage and salary inflation. We also know that Shimomura had for years a starring role on the policy board of the Bank of Japan. Fortunately anyone doing a deep study of the Japanese economic miracle—first rank economists such as such as Kenneth Bieda, Kenneth K Kurihara, and in more recent decades Richard A Werner —cannot fail to come across Shimomura or his works in their investigation. And the Development Bank of Japan has given Shimomura his due prominence as "Japan's most influential post-war economist" (see http://www.dbj.jp/ricf/fellowship/) even if they leave the key formulae out of the only DBJ-provided English translation of his major work.

There can be no doubt whatsoever that Shimomura was responsible for the key modification of Keynes' central investment-savings equilibrium condition to include no-cost investment credit created credit (by the BoJ) or low-cost long term debt (from the viewpoint of industrial borrowers) in that formula. That formula is there in a central pride of place in his Model of the Japanese Economy and its equations, as presented to the joint meeting of the Japanese Economic Association and the Japanese Econometric Society. His presentation was then published under the title "Seicho Seisaku No Kihon Mondai" (Basic Problems of Growth Policy) in Riron Keizaigaku, March 1961.

But it is now impossible to tell if Shimomura was responsible for the Japanese inflation-reducing policy of legislatively requiring wage and salary increases to be split, and partly awarded as an increase in weekly or monthly income and partly in November bonuses. Shimomura was in an official price-controlling position which implies he may have been responsible for the origin of that policy, but there is no available evidence to prove that he was. That treatment of income awards very significantly reduces the inflationary potential of consumer demand and stimulates long-term personal saving. I think the consummate cleverness of that policy may have Shimomura's fingerprints on it, but it seems that cannot now be proven.

The Tokyo Consensus as practiced during Japan's economic miracle years demonstrates how to achieve the successful management of national growth and inflation through a combination of measures which have a proven track record of success. The Washington Consensus has not similarly succeeded anywhere and its attempted adoption in Japan produced two decades of misery and economic stagnation which they call "their lost generation."

2.3.5 The United States of America 1938-44

No recent American Government has ever been (or needed to be) as focused as the FDR administrations were during the 1938-44 period, because the impending and actual world war required an intense focus which peacetime does not. The 32nd president, Franklin Delano Roosevelt, was an outstandingly intelligent man at the head of an amazingly fit-for-purpose Government which had the over-riding aim of ensuring that the allies would win the Second World War. The basic framework of US policy during that period was

1 No investment required by the war effort was to be held up for lack of funds

2 So the Fed and its 12 regional branches provided vast increases in investment credit creation to fund or create the industries, whose outputs were required to make the USA the "arsenal of the democracies" (and American industries successfully argued they were all in that category)

3 Wherever possible, industrialists were integrated into the process of national economic planning, but no roadblock to the achievement of economic victory was allowed to persist: non-cooperating industrialists were sidelined or ignored

4 The US government had no ideological objection to creating vast new industrial plants (for the production of steel and rubber, for instance)

5 Funds were also provided for required inventions and innovations (eg artificial rubber research and production, atomic bomb R&D, the continual stream of aircraft-improving innovations, etc)

6 Price control was very effectively carried out during part of that period by the Canadian economist John Kenneth Galbraith

7 All of the resources of the economy, all of its immigrants, and virtually all of its available workers (including the employment of many women) and most of its managers were enrolled in the planned production of higher US output and the associated economic development.The results of US wartime growth are a permanent part of world history. The USA grew at an average rate of 12.2% from 1938 to 1944, effectively doubling the size of the economy. Some of the highlights of that development are at http:// londonprogressivejournal.com/article/view/1507/fdrs-american-economic-miracle-or-the-first-economic-bomb-the-usa-from-to-part. Shimomuran economics, or investment credit economics, is as American as apple pie, and I mean the apple pie sold at McDonalds.

3 Conclusions

The Tokyo Consensus and the Shimomuran understandings on which it is based must be an absolute nightmare for the rightwing politicians of the West. A new and more successful economic understanding has blazingly emerged from Asia to challenge the old and well-established classical economic ideas "lest one good custom should corrupt the world." The wealth-creating combination of the government's power to create no-cost central bank credit and the canalisation of that credit through national and local banks to provide investment capital for major private businesses and millions of local SMEs is the most effective way to harness nearly all of the inventive and innovative talents of most of the creative people in an economy. Nothing else works as well.

When Thatcher won the first election victory in 1979, one of her election promises was that she would reverse British industrial decline, but she did nothing of the sort. Instead, she embraced the deadly simplicities of monetarism and regularly trumpeted the idea that "There is no alternative" to her policies. As Wikipedia notes (see http://en.wikipedia.org/wiki/There_is_no_alternative)

"There is no alternative (shortened as TINA) was a slogan often used by the Conservative British Prime Minister Margaret Thatcher. In economics, politics, and political economy, it has come to mean that "there is no alternative" to economic liberalism—that free markets, free trade, and capitalist globalization are the best or the only way for modern societies to develop."

But not only is there another way, "There Is A Much Better Way" or TIAMBA. The roots of the Tokyo Consensus, the bunch of economic understandings which I have called Shimomuran Economics, seem to have been originated by Franklin Delano Roosevelt in his administration's actions to ensure the American and Allied victories in the Second World War. These roots are impeccably American, democratic and helpful to all the workers of America. What I have christened as Shimomuran economics (because Shimomura was the first to explain it) was perhaps born as an astonishing piece of American know-how, providing no-cost-to-the-Fed investment credit creation debt to US industry to enable the greatest growth the American people have ever seen. And to place the USA in the position it still tentatively holds, as the greatest economic and military power in the world.

Neoclassical economics, on the other hand, is profoundly destructive to the wealth and welfare of the workers of not one in its homeland of America but also nearly everywhere else it is practised. It is profoundly undemocratic, capturing all media positions because it claims that it alone is the only true economic faith. And neo-classical economics has re-adopted Say's Law that unemployment is due to workers' wages not being sufficiently low, when unemployment is actually due to Government inaction which (among other things) denies the provision of sufficient investment credit, provided by a helpful banking system, to the 26.8 million SMEs which are a major foundation of American economic greatness and the prosperity of the American people. Michael Shaman's proposed policy of *Local Ownership, Import Substituting* is a similar answer [see Shuman, M. H. (2006) *The small-mart revolution: how local businesses are beating the global competition*, San Francisco, California, U.S.A.: Berrett-Koehler]. But America's SMEs do not just provide an answer to import substitution, they are the major source not only of much of the employment in the economy but also of most of inventions and a lot of innovation. From the small beginnings of SMEs mighty industries can grow. Neoclassical economics closes off many paths to the future because it is not supportive of invention and innovation, as Shimomuran economics is.

Shimomuran economics unlinks national economic growth from international finance. Governments do not need to borrow abroad to create an economic miracle once they understand Shimomuran Economics, for they can create wealth by requiring their Central Bank to create the credit to release the massive inventive and innovative talents of their people. None of the nations of the Tokyo consensus financed their economic miracles by foreign borrowing. Obama does not need to borrow from China. Neither does Merkel. The neoclassical mindset requires them to do so; the Tokyo consensus mindset doesn't.

Francis Fukuyama has argued in his 1992 book *The End of History and The Last Man* (Free Press. ISBN 0-02-910975-2) that liberal democracy has triumphed over all other existing political systems. The idea of liberal democracy has certainly triumphed but the reality of it has not. The western democracies have a marked tendency to turn into plutocracies serving only the interests of the rich and privileged, as most of their leading edge economies have done. Elections are sometimes run as exercises in political trickery with politicians promising policies which they either do not know how to deliver, or have no intention of delivering, once they are in office.

That tendency is most apparent in the United Kingdom, where an economically incompetent Coalition Government is implementing policies never mentioned in any of their manifestos, where each of the three main parties is committed in future to the similar deadly neoclassical economics of increasing family impoverishment and where the electoral response is to vote for a previously unknown party in the hope they might behave differently. I once thought no British governments could possibly be more destructive of domestic living standards than the Cameron-Clegg-Osborne Coalition Government, but UKIP now looks likely to be worse.

The mindset of the Tokyo Consensus zone is more productive than that of the Washington Consensus Zone. The rapidly increasing economic potential of China will in due course provide a hegemonic challenge to the USA and its allies which can only be met through the Western adoption of Shimomuran economics.

I have written to President Barack Obama several times in the hope he and his administration might listen, without success so far, and adopt Shimomuran economics. But the day may yet come...."

****

The clearest contrast between neoclassical economics and the Shimomuran-Wernerian high-growth, low-inflation economics being practised in the Tokyo Consensus Zone is given at the start of discussion in section 4.1 of Appendix 1, which is reproduced here for its relevance to the issue of why Western-trained economists are so practically useless:

"**4.1 Theoretical and Realistic Economics** There are two major traditions in economics, the theoretical and the realistic. The climax of theoretical economics and the mindset within which most Western trained economists are trapped is the castle in the air of neoclassical economics. As Wikipedia puts it "Neoclassical economics is also often seen as relying too heavily on complex mathematical models, such as those used in general equilibrium theory, without enough regard to whether these actually describe the real economy." The simple fact is that they don't. Wikipedia adds "A famous answer to this criticism is Milton Friedman's claim that theories should be judged by their ability to predict events rather than by the realism of their assumptions" [See http://en.wikipedia.org/wiki/ Neoclassical_economics]. But neoclassical economics has now been tried for over a third of a century throughout the entire Washington Consensus area and has utterly failed to produce the frequently predicted and promised prosperity, and has instead led to widespread misery. The dominance of the Anglosphere has enabled Washington economic advisors to push their unrealistic views down the throats of non-Western nations and has led to widespread derision about major Washington institutions (eg the IMF, World Bank, OECD etc.). Western politicians often appear quite crazy because they are usually acting in good faith from the best economic advice available to them from their neoclassical "experts". These politicians are pursuing policies which cannot possibly work but which have caused lost decades and an economic doldrums despite their highly developed economies and their inventive, innovative and well-educated people, because neoclassical economics does not adequately relate to the real world.

There is an alternative realistic economics, based upon the tradition of "the German Historical School of Economics" [See http:// en.wikipedia.org/wiki/Historical_school_of_economics]

That alternative focuses on a real-world historical analysis about what works and what is actually happening. As Wikipedia comments

"The historical school held that history was the key source of knowledge about human actions and economic matters, since economics was culture-specific, and hence not generalizable over space and time. The school rejected the universal validity of economic theorems. They saw economics as resulting from careful empirical and historical analysis instead of from logic and mathematics. The school also preferred reality, historical, political, and social, as well as economic, to mathematical modelling."

Wikipedia adds

"In the Anglosphere (English speaking countries), the historical school is perhaps the least known and least understood approach to the study of economics, because it differs radically from the now-dominant Anglo-American analytical point of view. Yet, the historical school forms the basis—both in theory and in practice—of the social market economy,[citation needed] for many decades the dominant economic paradigm in most countries of continental Europe.

The historical school is also a source of Joseph Schumpeter's dynamic, change-oriented, and innovation-based economics."

The major area in the world where the German Historical School of Economics prevails is the "Tokyo-sphere" or the Tokyo Consensus Zone where Shimomuran no-cost investment credit economics underlies the creation of economies of "abundant capital" [See https://medium.com/@georgetaitedwards/the-rough-guide-to-shimomuran-economics-e9dca42c6808]

Professor Richard Werner of Southampton University has extended the Shimomuran analysis by placing it into an overall credit-creation framework [see that framework at slide 23 of http://www.gresham.ac.uk/sites/default/files/richard_werner_-_gresham_college_3_mar_2015.pdf] and the most thorough example of modern realistic economics is Shimomuran-Wernerian macroeconomics."

It is horrifying to watch the entire culture of the Anglosphere decline in wealth and influence, under the malignant prescriptions of neoclassical macro-economics.

I know about several Ph D Students of economics that have set up secret study groups within their universities to study Shimomuran Economics. These groups have contacted me for some assistance but because there is no free speech in British Universities (all non-approved and non-neoclassical thought is banned by their lecturers) they have also requested that their existence and membership should remain secret. That ought to change.

There are "Common Responses to Shimomuran Economics" which I have listed at https://medium.com/@georgetaitedwards/common-responses-to-shimomuran-economics-d5a0b9f365ff which are completely relevant to this topic.

4.6 18th July 2014 "Why Western-Trained University Economists Are Almost Completely Useless"

"I have recently tried to communicate Shimomuran economics to several economists by attending the Rethinking Economics Conference London (held at 28-29 June at University College, London). I have also tried to communicate with many economists throughout the world, via the internet, and have found that the educational brainwashing of Western-trained economists is so great that they cannot usually think outside the mental box fitted by their university education.

Virtually all Western-trained economists have several completely wrong fixed ideas and this brief article deals with the major one which inhibits their understanding of rapid economic growth.

That major wrong idea is that national investment must be funded by either domestic saving or foreign borrowing. That fixed belief makes them unable to see some of the situations they are looking at and it often makes their commentaries on some Asian economies quite ridiculous.

An essay from the book "Showa—The Japan of Hirohito", edited by Carol Gluck and Stephen R Gruahard, Norton and Company, New York, 1992, illustrates the problem.

(See http://www.amazon.co.uk/Showa-Japan-Hirohito-Carol-Gluck/dp/0393310647/ref=sr_1_sc_1?ie=UTF8&qid=1368424747&sr=8-1-spell&keywords=Showa+-+The+Japan+of+Hirohita)

One of the fifteen essay contributors (Edward J Lincoln, the Senior Fellow at the Brookings Institute, Washington) makes this statements about high Japanese plant and equipment investment:

"The money for investment in plant and equipment must have come from somewhere in the form of savings. To say Japan was characterized by a high share of fixed capital formation in GDP implies that either Japan generated a high share of domestic savings or borrowed extensively from the rest of the world. Japan did not borrow heavily [in fact it did not borrow at all] from international capital markets, a feature that was reinforced by government policy in the high-growth years after the war (which essentially prohibited the private sector from borrowing abroad)."

p196, op. cit.

My additional text is in square brackets. He goes on to say:

"Therefore, high investment was funded by high domestic savings."

Absolutely wrong—high investment was mainly funded by credit creation at the Bank of Japan, about which Mr Lincoln appears to know nothing. The money came from somewhere, all right, because it was created by the Japanese Government as an act of monetary policy in the form of investment credit creation through the re-discounting of the pre-existing bank loans by the Bank of Japan— but that does not appear to be a possibility that the mindset of Mr Edward J Lincoln can allow.

Mr Edward J Lincoln is not alone in his wrong, and not fully informed, thinking. I could find similar statements in almost any basic economic textbook and it is often an unstated assumption in other economic papers. That mistaken logic forms the basis for many of the incorrect statements in the economic reports about some Asian nations, produced by Western institutions such as the IMF, the World Bank, the OECD etc. It also features in the national debt tables of the CIA World "Factbook," which lists the very real Greek government debts in the same table as Chinese and Japanese government "debts" (when these Asian "debts" are actually no-cost interest-receiving, income-generating assets as far as the central bank is concerned). The failure to discriminate between a debt (or money you owe to a third party it has been borrowed from) and an asset (or money owed to you by a third party, on which you are receiving interest) makes the CIA public debt tables at best misleading and at worst useless with regard to the Asian investment credit economies of Japan, China, South Korea and Taiwan, and perhaps several others.

The national government debt table in the CIA World "Factbook" should be reconstituted where required as two columns, one entitled "Government Domestic Assets" showing the loans created at the Central Bank for investment purposes (which are assets held by the Bank of Japan on behalf of the Japanese Government) and a "Government Debt" column showing the borrowings of the Government from third parties. I have written to the CIA saying so, but perhaps my advice on this issue may not be entirely welcome. The highly qualified Western-educated recipients of the advice probably could not understand what I was saying. Still, these tables need correction, preferably soon.

Part of the confusion was created by the administration of Franklin Delano Roosevelt, which wrote down the balancing entry for the American 1938-44 investment credit creation as "The savings of the people" although the people had nothing to do with it. Other credit-creating governments have followed suit. Maybe less people should believe what they read and more people should investigate what they are being told.

Western economists need to recognise the fact that investment credits can appear in the economy as if it were foreign investment, created by the credit-creating activities of the Central Bank. These new credits are better than foreign investment because they are not narrowly focused on investments to provide exported output (as foreign investments usually are). Furthermore, these new funds can help all the industries and SMEs in a country, they do not create ownership by, and a stream of future repayments to, foreigners, and they have generally widespread and helpful economic effects, creating a country of abundant capital as in occurring in all the nations of the Tokyo Consensus and which could happen everywhere if Western and world economists brightened up. (A country of abundant capital is my generalisation of Shinzo Abe's choice phrase "A Japan of Abundant Capital" as part of his vision for the future of Japan.)

The central investment-funding equation of the Shimomura Model of the Japanese economy is

$Is + Id = S + D$ (Equation [3.1])

Or Is (Investment financed by saving) plus Id (Investment financed by debt) equals Saving (S) plus Debt (D, equal to investment credit created by investment credit at creation at the Bank of Japan).

That is, the investment level of Japan is increased by credit creation at the Central Bank of Japan. This equation replaces the classic and central Keynesian Savings-Investment equality with a more useful formula because (if the nation's banks give a high priority to commercial and industrial investment) the government of a country can increase the nation's investment level through investment credit creation at the Central Bank. So no-cost investment credit, created by the Bank of Japan, once transmitted through a co-operative banking system to industry, creates vast flows of additional wealth through industrial investment, higher employment and the continually updated production of better goods and services.

Kenneth Kenkichi Kurihara has produced the central insight of his

understanding of the Shimomura model in the immortal words:
"In the light of such financial arrangements in Japan as described by
equations (1.1)—(1.5) it is not at all surprising that Shimomura
should make a seemingly paradoxical reference to Japan's 'rate of
(capital) accumulation remaining very high despite her rising
consumption level.' (1) If, therefore, greater investment can be
financed partly by credits, there is no need for that 'abstinence'
which the classical economists considered necessary for economic
progress, any more than there is for that 'austerity' which some
present day underdeveloped countries impose on already under-
consuming populations at the constant peril of social unrest. Nor is it
difficult, in such credit-creating circumstances, to agree with Keynes'
observation that investment and consumption should be regarded as
complementary rather than competitive." (2)
1 Shimomura, "Basic Problems in Growth Policy", Economic
Studies Quarterly, March 1961.
2 Kurihara, Applied Dynamic Economics, George Allen and Unwin,
London, 1963, p61.
Why have Western economists ignored the fundamental insights of
Dr Osamu Shimomura, who the Bank of Japan has referred to as
"Japan's most influential post war economist"? A large part of the
reason for that is because many Western economists think they have
a perfect understanding, that they know everything, and their
discipline is on a par with Physics. But the Tokyo Consensus nations
know one of the most important things in economics—about how to
create an economic explosion, how to convert an economy from
peasantry to industrial power within a few decades, and there are
four major examples of that process in Japan, China, South Korea
and Taiwan—and the above equation is the secret of that.
During the last fifty years I have frequently been told that these
fresh-to-the-West Shimomuran insights are wrong. The Japanese
have a lovely expression which covers that response. They smile
sweetly and say
"If you believe or not".
In other words, if you do not accept reality, events will educate you
where your education and your prejudices have failed.
The major reason for the hole in the heart of Western economics
teaching—by which I mean the absence of teaching of any
prescription for the acceleration of economic growth—is because
Western universities don't teach Shimomuran economics. They

should. In terms of a physics analogy, western economists understand the equivalent of Newtonian physics, while some of their Asian counterparts understand Einstein's atomics. The West does not understand how to make economic explosions, the East does. Western university teaching should include Shimomuran economics in the curriculum as soon as possible, and Western economists should realise there is a third source of investment funding—credit creation by the central bank—which could greatly assist US and EU recovery if they understood it."

4.7 20th December 2013 "Shimomuran Economics is the Most Significant Advance Ever Made in Economic Understanding and the West Still Doesn't Get It"

This article was originally published on Friday 20th December 2013 at http://londonprogressivejournal.com/article/view/1688/ shimomuran-economics-is-the-most-significant-advance-ever-made-in-economic-understanding-and-the-west-still-doesnt-get-it and republished on August 4th 2014 at: https://medium.com/ @georgetaitedwards/shimomuran-economics-is-the-most-significant-advance-ever-made-in-economic-understanding-and-the-e540e58bf270

"1 An Introduction to Shimomuran Economics

Shimomuran economics is the name I have given to the collection of no-debt, high-growth economic understandings practised in post-war Japan and post-rapprochement China. Technically that economics—investment credit economics—was invented by the third administration of Franklin Delano Roosevelt in about 1937, and was based (as it still is) on the fundamental economic principles set out by John Maynard Keynes in the General Theory and The Tract on Monetary Reform and elsewhere as briefly explained in paragraph 3 below. But Shimomura studied what the Americans had done and not only did he persuade Japanese politicians and bankers to practice his fresh high-growth economics, but also he set out, developed and published (in Japanese) the main principles of an investment credit creation (or ICC) economy in several locations.

Shimomuran economics is therefore the same as the Rooseveltian economics which won the Second World War for the Allies by producing the explosive economic growth of America from 1938-44, when the USA doubled its economic output. It is the Shimomuran understandings set out in his seminal book "Seicho Seisaku No Kihon Mondai" (*Basic Problems of Growth Policy* in Riron Keizaigaku, March 1961) which propelled Japan, in the course of a few decades, from being an impoverished war-damaged economy into one of the major industrial economies of the world. And the adoption of Shimomuran economics in China has produced the largest economic miracle and potentially the major preponderant superpower of the 21st century.

According to the Development Bank of Japan, Dr Osamu Shimomura (1910-89), who was the "Father of the Japanese economic miracle" also "rose to become Japan's most influential post war economist, founding a school of thought based on the "Shimomura Theory," which attracted numerous followers" and "Dr Shimomura was well known for the development of a theory of economic growth based on a dynamic view of Keynesian economics."

See **http://www.dbj.jp/ricf/en/fellowship/**

2 What Shimomuran Economics is

Shimomuran economics is new branch of high-growth, low-inflation macro-economics. It is a direct development of Keynesian Economics. It almost certainly had its beginnings from Shimomura's observation of the Rooseveltian practise of investment credit creation in the USA during the 1938-44 period, which it resembles in every respect. It was implemented in Japan from 1945, in order to restore the prosperity of Japan after the devastation of World War II, and was further developed into an explicit economic model by Dr Osamu Shimomura (1910-1989) between 1946 and 1961. Shimomuran economics was intended to provide Japan with a semi-permanent trading advantage, based upon abundant, low-repayment-cost capital for investment in private industry, and it succeeded magnificently in doing that for decades. Shinzo Abe is trying once more to reintroduce Shimomuran economics into Japan after the disastrous attempt by the "Princes of the Yen" to follow Washington Consensus economics after the collapse of the Japanese asset bubble. After a "lost generation" in Japan, caused entirely by the wrong-headed attempt to "restructure" Japan along Washington Consensus lines, Japan is now re-establishing the economic systems which founded Japan's first post war economic miracle.

3 The Three Keynesian Foundations of Shimomuran Economics

Shimomuran Economics is the natural development from three of Keynes' observations. These three are set out below.3.1 **"While there are intrinsic reasons for the shortage of land, there are no intrinsic reasons for the shortage of capital"** J M Keynes, "The General Theory…" Book 6, Chapter 24, Section 2, p.376

3.2 "Saving can be created in advance of the return on investments which justify it.." These observations are fundamental to the practice of Shimomuran economics. Or as Kenneth Bieda has written:

"The Japanese monetary policy, in fact, applied one of the Keynesian principles: saving does not have to precede investment in conditions where there is unemployment, but investment acts financed by bank-created money can precede savings."

Kenneth Bieda, The Structure and Operation of the Japanese Economy, John Wiley and Sons Australasia Pty Ltd, Sydney, 1970.

3.3 Central Banks can purchase no-debt assets by making claims against themselves In the Tract on Monetary Reform Keynes recognised that a Central Bank "may itself purchase assets, i.e. add to its investments, and pay for them, in the first instance at least, by establishing a claim against itself."
J M Keynes, Tract on Monetary Reform, p. 21

This is exactly what the Central Banks of all the "economic miracle" countries have done (the USA 1938-44, Japan 1946-75, China mid-1970s to now) and they do not simply do this in the first instance but over decades, as a deliberate act of long-term economic policy. The assets created at the Central Bank do not need to be sold to the financial markets or sourced by foreign or domestic borrowing. If these created credits were debts, they would need to be financed, but as they are assets, no borrowing to support them is necessary, although a fictional entry of "savings of the people" is usually generated to preserve the double-entry nature of national bookkeeping.

3.4 The irrefutability of Shimomuran Economics All of the above three statements are obvious and undeniable. There are no intrinsic reasons for the shortage of capital, "saving" or investment credit can be and has been created in advance of the returns which justify it, and central banks can, and have, created credit by discounting pre-existing loans, buying these assets from the banks, by establishing a no-cost "done in the public interest" claim against themselves.

4 The Practice and Objectives of Shimomuran Economics

Shimomuran Economics is therefore based upon no-debt Investment Credit Creation at the Central Bank, where credit is canalised through the national banking system to long-term, low-cost loans for all kinds of private industry in every part of the country, in order to create a long-term boom in capital investment and widespread prosperity as evidenced by high and continually increasing productivity, in a full employment, high wages and excellent social benefits economy.

Dr Osamu Shimomura replaced the I=S Keynesian Investment-Saving equation with a more useful formulation in his Model of the Japanese Economy (published 1961, under the title "Seicho Seisaku No Kihon Mondai" (Basic Problems of Growth Policy) in Riron Keizaigaku, March 1961) by specifying the more dynamic equation

$I_s + I_d = S + D$ where
I_s = Investment financed by Saving
I_d = Investment financed by Debt
S=Saving and
D=Debt

This produces the prime equation for an exploding economy in which investment vastly exceeds saving or $I \gg S$ due to investment credit creation with its initial impetus in the Bank of Japan.

Dr Shinohara, at first a critic and doubtful advocate of the Shimomura insights, became a strong but appraising supporter, publishing "The Secret of Accelerated Growth" in late 1961. Shinohara in particular disagreed with Shimomura's prediction of 10% pa economic growth in Japan during the 1960s and thought the 7.2% pa forecast by Japan's Economic Planning Agency was likely to more correct. Economic growth in 1960s Japan turned out closer to the Shimomuran forecast than the EPA one, and the prestige of the economist Dr Osamu Shimomura (1910-1989) increased within Japan accordingly, with the great doctor becoming the leading economic advisor to the 1960s Ikeda adminstration. Or as the Development Bank of Japan puts it at their Website:

"Dr. Shimomura was well known for the development of a theory of economic growth based on a dynamic view of Keynesian economics.

In the early postwar period, he was convinced of the value of the
technological innovation then being produced and in the late 1950s
entered the controversy over economic growth with a theory of high-
rate economic growth. Applying a historical perspective to the
postwar Japanese economy, Dr. Shimomura was the first to
accurately predict the coming period of sustained high-rate economic
growth. In the 1960s, Dr. Shimomura served as a top economic
policy adviser in the Ikeda administration and helped set in place the
income-doubling plan."

This quotation is from the DBJ website at **http://www.dbj.jp/ricf/
en/fellowship/**

So Shimomura was a Keynesian basing his understandings on the
dynamic recasting of the Keynesian economics by the great English
economist Sir Henry Roy Forbes Harrod (see **http://
en.wikipedia.org/wiki/Roy_Harrod)** and the Russian-American
economist Evsey Domar (1914-1997—see **http://en.wikipedia.org/
wiki/Evsey_Domar)** who both independently developed the Harrod-
Domar model (see **http://en.wikipedia.org/wiki/Harrod
%E2%80%93Domar_model)** on which Shimomura's "Model of
Japanese Economy" is solidly based, with the crucial modification of
the savings-investment dynamic equilibrium, as set out above, at its
centre.

5 The major effects of Shimomuran Economics

Shimomuran economics, considered in the round, has six major
effects, First, it drafts the unemployed into the capital goods sector,
converting labour (which would otherwise run to waste) into capital
goods to enrich the operation of the economy and the wealth of the
nation. Second, it provides the funds to continually modernise the
plant and equipment in the key capital goods sector and in all other
sectors of the economy by regularly increasing the level and the
quality of the capital investment at the elbow of the already working
population. Third, produces the essential upskilling of the employed
by funding the necessary training to enable the operation of the
continually-updated production machinery. Fourth, it funds and
accelerates the rate of invention in universities and laboratories and
the research and development in companies. Fifth, it funds the fresh
innovations (which are the embodiment of inventions into the

updated equipment on the factory floor and in the offices of the service industries of the economy) which drive economic growth forever upward. Finally, it provides the vast flows of no-cost, long term capital which enables governments to fund major capital-intensive projects to enrich the nation, and to cope with the increasing incidence of national disasters by providing timely and appropriate capital investment to protect the lives and assets of the nation and to replace assets lost through such major events and hence assist a faster recovery from any damage done.

So, in brief, Shimomuran economics:

a) Enables full employment
b) Improves labour productivity through higher investment in new and existing facilities
c) Provides upskilling of the workforce through training
d) Funds higher invention and R&D
e) Funds innovation and increases economic growth
f) Assists government by providing the capital funds for major projects and to provide the restorative capital required in the aftermath of national disasters.

Shinzo Abe certainly knows all this, as does the Chinese premier Li Keqiang. Why doesn't Cameron? Why doesn't Merkel? Why doesn't Obama?

Ruskin was absolutely right when he said "There is no wealth but life." The number and skills of the people in a nation and the level of equipment provided at the workplace to practice these skills determines the final boundary level of national income. The full use of the best skills of all the available people—full employment for all the working population operating at the highest level of skill each can attain, employing the best up-to-date equipment to maximise warranted output—is the route to the maximisation of national wealth.

Governments can channel national capital investment into key directions—into better green technologies, as Obama has, or into an attempt to bring about a society of "Good Health and Longevity" as Shinzo Abe has. Or they can just pointlessly blunder about, aimlessly wittering on about the need to make economies because of the inherited fiscal position of the government, as all the useless Cabinet members of the British Coalition Government currently do.

The government of each country has a duty of care towards the majority of its population. That is what democracy implies. Many Western governments are failing to practice their duty of care. The cost-cutting, austerity-practising economies of the West are chasing the recession down into a spiral of permanent loss. The waste of lives, the loss of labour output which can never be recovered, the damage to the personal lives of the people through an unnecessary austerity, the destruction by increased poverty of their personal "golden hours, each set with sixty diamond minutes", the foolish and appalling impoverishment of families, the unnecessary suffering brought about by confusing economics with economies by politicians who ought to know better, should all become things of the past.

Shimomuran economics provides the road to national riches where politicians understand it. At present, only a few do understand it but that dawning light is sure to illuminate the future of mankind for it is, in Scott Fitzgerald's memorable words "the diamond that is bigger than the Ritz".

At present, Britain would be better economically managed if it became the 24th province of China than it is being managed by the current Coalition government. The programme of cuts are endless and pointless. The economic stupidity of Cameron and Osborne, running the economy only for the benefit of the rich, and selling part of Britain's future—the generation of electricity from atomic power —to China, cannot be justified. It is a deal which needs to be undone from a Government that needs to be voted out of office. The creation of credit at the Bank of England and the provision of that credit to British or European energy generation investors to serve the same purpose, is a much better Shimomuran solution, and that solution should be applied to all British industries. The economies practising Shimomuran economics are going to dominate the future of the world, because only they will be the most innovative and prosperous.

Only Shimomuran economics provides a solution to the credit crunch. Western politicians are sure to eventually realise that. Western economists, following as usual in the train of political action, will eventually adopt Shimomuran economics so thoroughly that they will pretend to forget they ever thought otherwise.

Shimomuran economics fulfils the Keynesian objective of making economists as "useful as dentists"—providing effective remedies to the pains of poverty and a future ease of richer living to most of the population. It could even give some currently vilified bankers a useful role in the economic progress of the country. Competent politicians would have the starring role. But they would all need to understand Shimomuran economics first, and in the West and at the minute, they don't get it.

This article has been written with the intention of improving their economic understanding and in the hope that they might get it, soon.

They eventually will, one way or another. This issue is never going to go away, nor should it. The promulgation of this understanding is one of the central issues of my life.

As a Scot, I was brought up with the story of Bruce and the spider, illustrating the value of never surrendering any viewpoint which is right. Lately, I too have been further inspired by Shinzo Abe's telling of the story of Ino Tadataka, who said:

"No matter how difficult a challenge may seem, it is always possible to overcome it provided you have a strong will never to give up.There is no such thing as "too late" to take action."

Politicians and economists please note.

Note 1 : I have published a book about "Shimomuran Economics" at http://www.lulu.com/shop/george-tait-edwards/shimomuran-economics/paperback/product-21688864.html and much else elsewhere during the last four decades. His sixth book, "Lucky Bastards of the 20th Century-The Story of the Economic Bomb" can be found at http://www.lulu.com/shop/george-tait-edwards/lucky-bastards-of-the-20th-century/paperback/product-21913362.html.

Note 2: This article, which has been slightly updated, was first published in the London Progressive Journal on Friday 20th December 2013 at http://londonprogressivejournal.com/article/view/1688/shimomuran-economics-is-the-most-significant-advance-ever-made-in-economic-understanding-and-the-west-still-doesnt-get-it.

It is a key article which needs to be fully appreciated by its readers, and I hope and intend it will be."

4.8 11th March 2015 "Dr Osamu Shimomura's Major Achievements"

This article was published on March 11 2015 at https://medium.com/ @georgetaitedwards/dr-osamu-shimomura-1910-89-his-major-achievements-be2ad3e39e77

"One of the comments I received in the lead-up to the Gresham College Spring 2015 Long Finance Conference (see http:// www.gresham.ac.uk/the-curious-case-of-japan-why-macroeconomics-needs-a-rethink) was from one individual who said "I am not sure of exactly what Shimomura did!" This is an expanded article version of my emailed reply to him.

What Dr Osamu Shimomura did was:
1 Shimomura explained the economic policy which makes high economic growth possible
There have been six investment credit economies where very high economic growth has occurred.

These "miracle economies" are

1.1 Japanese-occupied Manchuria during the 1930s (see http:// www.japansociety.org.uk/20591/the-comprehensive-history-of-south-manchurianrailways-company-%E6%BA %80%E9%89%84%E5%85%A8%E5%8F%B2/)

1.2 the USA from 1938–44 (see http://londonprogressivejournal.com/ article/view/1507/fdrs-american-economic-miracle-or-the-first-economic-bomb-the-usa-from-to-part)

1.3 Japan from 1945–75 (see http://londonprogressivejournal.com/ article/view/1566/the-origin-of-shimomuras-japanese-economic-miracle-or-the-second-economic-bomb-japan-from-to-economic-miracles-part)

1.4 South Korea from the 1960s (for a brief consideration of the four Asian "Tigercub economies" see see pages 39–42 of "Lucky Bastards of the 20th Century—The Story of the Economic Bomb" showcased at https://medium.com/@georgetaitedwards/lucky-bastards-of-the-20th-century-8bd352881b6b)

1.5 Taiwan also from the 1960s (also see the reference at 4 above)

1.6 China from the late 1970s to the present day (see http://londonprogressivejournal.com/article/view/1622/chinas-allinclusive-economic-miracle-the-third-economic-bomb)

The last four of these economies constitute the Tokyo Consensus Zone, where Shimomuran economics is understood and practised. See https://medium.com/@georgetaitedwards/a-comparison-of-the-washington-berlin-and-tokyo-consensus-zones-221e7e53018b
The only 20th century economist who has competently explained how very high growth occurs in Japan has been Dr Osamu Shimomura, who set out the first explicit Harrod-Domar "economic model of Japan' which takes into account no-cost investment credit creation (of about c15% pa of GDP) at the central bank (or the BoJ) as a source of funds aimed at significantly accelerating economic growth. See https://medium.com/@georgetaitedwards/the-master-economist-2a744a336ece
If any Japanese economist in Manchuria had explained how that economic miracle had occurred, this fresh high-growth economics might have been called "Manchurian economics." If FDR in the USA or his major economic advisor John Kenneth Galbraith had explained what they were doing this macroeconomics might have been christened "Rooseveltian economics" or "Galbraithian economics". Only Shimomura took the trouble to explain how the Japanese government's high growth policy actually worked so I have christened this fresh branch of high-growth, low-inflation macro-economics as "Shimomuran Economics". But in view of Professor Richard Werner's recent meticulous analysis of the relationships between credit creation by the Bank of Japan and economic outcomes, this fresh-to-the-West macroeconomics is most accurately referred to as "Shimomuran-Wernerian macroeconomics." See https://medium.com/p/why-do-you-refer-to-investment-credit-economics-as-shimomuran-economics-if-it-was-first-d18779170617
which repeats some of the above observations.

2 He modified Keynes' savings-investment equilibrium and suggested what the annual level of BoJ investment Credit Creation should be

Dr Osamu Shimomura not only proposed a modified Keynesian savings-investment equilibrium but also he made the specific suggestion that these funds can add 15% of GDP annually to the national investment level (and, with a capital-output ratio of 3, about 5% pa to economic growth pa). He did this in 1961 on the basis of his previous experience with post-war BoJ credit creation. No-one anywhere else has done that, although the model is actually not only consistent with the Domar-Harrod dynamic recasting of Keynesianism but also it probably provides the fundamental equations which support of the central ideas of modern monetary theory.

3 He suggested how wage and salary increases could be paid in stages to reduce potential inflation While acting in the Price Control administration of the Bank of Japan, Shimomura successfully promoted the idea (which became part of the Japanese "Spring Income Offensive" wage and salary negotiations) that annual negotiated wage and salary increases should be awarded in two stages—with about half of the annual percentage increase adding to weekly or monthly wages and the other half being paid as a lump sum bonus during the first week in November. This was (and probably is) the most effective method of reducing potential inflation rates [while permitting continual living standards increases] yet devised, because it halves the money increase available to consumers for immediate expenditure each year, and Japanese Economic Planning Agency research (reported in the EPA's Economic Survey of Japan) has demonstrated that lump sum bonuses paid in November were more likely to be saved, providing (in an investment credit economy) more security for families based on higher savings and more bank funds for potentially productive investment.

4 He recalculated the multiplier as having a different value depending upon where new money enters the monetary expenditure cycle Shimomura's 1962 book *Economic Fluctuation and Multiplier Analysis* analyses the multiplier into different values depending on the origin of the monetary impulse and provides estimates of these "multipliers" values for 1960s Japan. The Keynesian multiplier is usually calculated as a single number, and whether the extra funds are injected into the expenditure cycle as consumer spending, or into SMEs and companies as investment credit, the total monetary expansion is alleged to be the same. [Even the master economist Kenneth Kurihara estimates a single multiplier, equal to the inverse of the propensities to save and to tax and to import on p 70 of his book "The Growth Potential of the Japanese Economy" The John Hopkins Press, Baltimore and London, 1971.] But Shimomura's 1962 book argues this is not so, and that it is possible to selectively increase the income of industrial companies without producing a great effect on demand, because investment expenditure is a firm-to-firm payment which is only incurred as new plant and equipment investments are put into place and paid for. This is the work that earned Shimomura his doctorate, and although the estimates of the real value of the multiplier has been performed for many economies, none of these is as specific as this book, because none of them appear to have related the different values of the multiplier to the point in the monetary cycle where the funds are injected.

5 He was a major player in bringing about the Japanese Economic Miracle Dr Shimomura's friendship with Hiyato Ikeda lasted for decades, as he was at first a friend and colleague of Ikeda when both both worked in the MoF (1934–47) then as a supportive colleague when Ikeda became first, Deputy Minister of Finance (1947–49) then Minister of Finance (1949–52) and ultimately Prime Minister (1960–64), a term tragically cut short by Ikeda's laryngeal cancer in 1964. Shimomura is acknowledged in many Japanese sources as "the brains behind the Ikeda Administration" but the inadequate obituary-description of Ikeda's life in Wikipedia lacks any reference to Dr O Shimomura:

"Takafusa Nakamura, a leading economic historian, described Ikeda as "the single most important figure in Japan's rapid growth. He should long be remembered as the man who pulled together a national consensus for economic growth." His plan predicted a 7.2 percent growth rate (thereby doubling GNP over ten years), but by the second half of the 1960s, average growth had climbed to an astounding 11.6%. In addition, while Ikeda's "income-doubling plan" called for average personal incomes to double with ten years, this was actually achieved within seven years.[8] "

6 He calculated economic growth rates from his practical knowledge of capital-output ratios In 1958–9, Shimomura took specific issue with the EPA's income doubling plan and suggested that a 10% pa growth rate was achievable by Japan during the 1960s and that the 7.2% forecast was therefore too low. This observation ignited Japan's 1960s "growth controversy" with many prominent economists (particularly his superior in the Ministry of Finance, who became Professor Mikoyei Shinohara) supporting the EPA prediction as more likely. But Shimomura had done his research and he knew the capital-output ratios of virtually every part of Japanese manufacturing industry, and the 1960s Japanese growth results turned out to be 10.2% pa.

During the first half of the 1960s, Japanese economic growth turned out to have a midway value of about 8.4% pa, which suggested that both the EPA forecast and Shimomura had a case for their predictions. But during the second half of the 1960s Japan's growth rate soared to about 11.6% pa, producing a total factor increase of about 2.64 or about an average GDP growth of 10.2% pa for the whole decade.

7 Shimomura continually supported the subsidiarity of the Bank of Japan (BoJ) to the Ministry of Finance. He powerfully agued that the BoJ must not be independent but must be a servant in the delivery of investment credit to the secondary banks for onwards transmission through local banks to SMEs and manufacturing industry. He won all of these encounters. See page 24 of The Political Economy of Japanese Monetary Policy, Thomas Cargill and others, The MIT Press, Cambridge, Massachusetts and London, with page 24 also available to review on the internet at http://books.google.co.uk/books?id=f3s47HWB8g8C&printsec=frontcover&source=gbs_ge_summary_r&cad=0#v=onepage&q&f=false

8 Shimomura continually changed his policy recommendations with changing circumstances Shimomura calculated the declining productivity of Japanese capital investment (which the increasing capital-output trend illustrated) and as a counterpart to his predictions of high growth in his 1963 book, produced a 1976 book "Conditions for escaping from zero growth." He explained that national economic policies should be continually updated to reflect changing circumstances and his book titles reflect these changing priorities. See, for example, the article at http://fukushimanewsresearch.wordpress.com/2011/08/01/japan-weighing-economic-growth-against-nuclear-risks-makes-no-sense/

and the book titles listed at https://medium.com/@georgetaitedwards/
there-are-now-three-books-by-dr-osamu-shimomura-1910-1989-in-
the-national-library-of-e4f34c351402

**9 The effective interest rate on new or discounted investment
credit funds at the Bank of Japan was set equal to the measured
inflation rate of factory gate goods** That policy maximises
economic development by making money a counterpart of real
resources and while making long-term capital cheap, ensures it is not
free.

Conclusions

These nine major contributions or how-to-do-it demonstrations to
economic thought and practise are more than enough to place Dr
Osamu Shimomura among the pantheon of the world's master
economists. The significance of each of these contributions is, in my
view

1 That he explained the "secret" of Japanese economic growth better
than anyone else did during the 20th century

2 That he was not content with just a "theory of (Japanese) economic
growth" but he also specified the numbers which he thought should
be applied within the model

3 That he explained how the major inflation-producing effect of
annual consumer wage and salary increases could be reduced while
maintaining high wage and salary increases, improving household
savings, bank deposits and economic stability at the same time

4 That he explained how the injection of investment capital into
firms and SMEs need not result in high inflation (because high
liquidity and the slower introduction of major projects reduces the
multiplier, as does the paying of wage and salary awards in two
tranches)

5 That he was not content to be a theoretical economist, he was (like
J M Keynes and J K Galbraith) a major player in helping politicians
to bring about high economic growth

6 That his economic understanding was founded on realistic
estimates of capital-output ratios based in turn on personal
knowledge and practical research

7 That he understood how Central Banks could not be trusted to
behave in the interests of the nation and had to be obedient to
national political control, and that this could only be achieved
through CB subsidiarity to the Ministry of Finance

8 Like J M Keynes, he was not a one-trick pony—he readjusted his economic views with changing circumstances and in the presence of new information, and

9 An appropriate interest cost of capital funds was set to maximise economic development and stabilise the system.

Other people might pick a different set of achievements, and the above list is inevitably a personal view. Dr Osamu Shimomura's investment credit creation high-growth low-inflation macroeconomics is not a theoretical mathematic castle in the air, as neoclassical economics is. His macroeconomics is more like Watt's snorting steam engine because both are based on the calculated numerical realities of life.

And Shimomuran-Wernerian macroeconomics has an immense advantages over neoclassical economics. It produces the goods, it finances a much higher level of conversion of invention to innovation, it results in more rapid economic progress and widespread prosperity in the countries which practice it. But that is better discussed in a separate article.

The nations of the West are paying an immense price of widespread social misery, economic decline and a reduction in cultural influence due to their allegiance to an outdated political macroeconomics which does not produce the goods. It is difficult to know how long that will continue, but it cannot continue for much longer.

We are all just as poor as our economists are ineffective and our politicians are unresponsive. The economies of the West could continue to decline much further against that touchstone.

Note 1: George Tait Edwards has published a first sequence of collected articles in a book about "Shimomuran Economics" available at http://www.lulu.com/shop/george-tait-edwards/ shimomuran-economics/paperback/product-21688864.html and much else elsewhere during the last four decades. Also see "The Rough Guide to Shimomuran Economics" at https://medium.com/ @georgetaitedwards/the-rough-guide-to-shimomuran-economics-e9dca42c6808 and the showcased cover summary and prologue of that sixth book at https://medium.com/@georgetaitedwards/lucky-bastards-of-the-20th-century-8bd352881b6b and consider the purchase of that sixth book which is called "Lucky Bastards of the 20th Century- The Story of the Economic Bomb" which can be found at http://www.lulu.com/shop/george-tait-edwards/lucky-

bastards-of-the-20th-century/paperback/product-21913362.html.
Note 2: Some of the articles and discussion on this topic can be
accessed at http://londonprogressivejournal.com/user/view/2285 as
well as through my two recent books referenced above.

4.9 3rd March 2015 "The Curious Case of the Economist the West Forgot"- a lecture at Gresham College

Slide 1 - The cover of Shimomura's best biography

This is an image of "Japan's most influential post-war economist" Dr Osamu Shimomura (1910-89) on the book cover of his best biography "Omoi yokoshimo nashi: Shimomura Osamu to gekido no Showa keizai" or "Thoughts that bear no evil" (Japanese) by Yo Mizuki, Tankobon Hardcover, 1992.

The lecture text follows below:

"This is the story of the economic bomb, about the discovery and spread of the new knowledge about how to make an economy grow with explosive force. This is the curious story of the man who explained how to build that economic bomb, the economist the West forgot, the Asian Keynes, whose writings and understandings the West has ignored. And perhaps above all, this is the story about the opening of a fresh path to prosperity for all mankind based upon a better macroeconomic understanding.

Since 1971 I have had an abiding interest in the economic policies and government procedures which produce explosive economic growth, particularly these set out and practised by the Japanese master economist Dr Osamu Shimomura (27 November 1910-29 June 1989), because his economic understanding lies at the root of the four high growth Tokyo Consensus economies - Japan, South Korea, Taiwan, and China (see note 1 below). These four countries have used and are using the superior economic understanding of Shimomuran macroeconomics to great effect.

Please relax and enjoy this lecture, which will be published on the Gresham College website (For this lecture with slides please see http://www.gresham.ac.uk/sites/default/files/ 03mar15longfinance_georgetaitedwardsfinal.pdf)

References are given in the notes at the end of this lecture. In this seminar I am going to address five questions:

Outline of Lecture

1. **Who was Dr Osamu Shimomura, economist, 1910-89**
2. **What did he do?**
3. **Why is that significant?**
4. **Why does the West ignore him?**
5. **How long could that continue?**

Slide 2 - lecture outline

Incidentally, if you search for "Dr Osamu Shimora" on the internet these days, most of the references are to the same-named Nobel Prize winner for his work on the phenomenon of bioluminescence. A search including the birth and death dates of 1910-89, produces results relating to Shimomura the economist.

Many of the facts about Shimomura are set out at the Development Bank of Japan (DBJ) website (where DBJ offer a "Shimomuran Fellowship" in honour of Japan's "most influential post-war economist" (see note 2 below).

The timeline of Dr Osamu Shimomura's life

Year	Activity
1910	Born in Saga Prefecture, Kyushu, Japan, on 27th November 1910
1930-34	Student in Economics Faculty, Tokyo Imperial University
1934	Joined Japanese Ministry of Finance (MoF)
1936	Sent by MoF to New York for economic research
1938	Worked in and studied South Manchurian Railway Company (the "Mantetsu")
1945	Visited USA as part of US-Japanese Businessmen Exchange Programme
1946-59	Manager in Price Bureau of the MoF
1960-66	Senior Executive Director of the Development Bank of Japan (DBJ)
1964-74	First Executive Director of DBJ's Research Institute of Capital Formation
1975-79	Chairman of the Japan Economic Research Institute (JERI)
1989	Died 29th June 1989

Slide 3 Timeline of Dr Shimomura's Life

One major aspect of Shimomura's life was that he was an activist, with four ways to affect Japanese economic policy - first, through his price-control position in the Japanese Ministry of Finance (MoF); second, in his advisory role on the BoJ Board; third, through his lengthy friendship with Hayato Ikeda (who was by turns his colleague in the MoF, the Japanese Minister of Finance and the Japanese Prime Minister); and finally through his persuasive written papers (such as the Income-Doubling Plan) and his dozen books and scores of other papers.

The *Mantetsu*, or South Manchurian Railway Company

1. **This debt-funded company and colony resulted from the Japanese defeat of the Russians in 1905 and the Treaty of Portsmouth**
2. **Operated by the Japanese Military**
3. **During the 1930s, Shinzo Abe's grandfather oversaw the development of the Mantetsu**
4. **Perhaps the most successful high-growth colony in history**
5. **During the 1920s, the Mantetsu provided over a quarter of Japanese Government tax revenues**
6. **The world's fist Investment Credit Creation economy**

Slide 4 - The Mantetsu

Shimomura studied and worked in the South Manchurian Railway Company (the Mantetsu) - and the post-war economic miracle in Japan was run by returning Japanese who were referred to as "the Manchurians" as most of these had been previously employed in the Mantetsu.

The Mantetsu (see notes 3 and 4) can be seen in retrospect as the testbed where the managers of the Japanese economic miracle cut their teeth. Shimomura knew all about how the Mantetsu operated, and it is interesting to note that Shinzo Abe's grandfather oversaw the Mantetsu development in Manchuria during the 1930s (see note 5).

Three major and different kinds of financial-industrial systems

1. **The Washington Consensus Zone,** where restrictive monetarism reigns supreme and is a dominant aspect of national cultures
2. **The Berlin Consensus Zone of the Industrial Banking Economies** where some public banks (ie the Sparkassen) collect large flows of saving and provide long-term finance for SME investment, i.e. in Germany
3. **The Tokyo Consensus Zone of the Investment Credit Creation (Shimomuran) Economies** where (during the last 70 or so years) government credit creation at the central bank is canalised via i intermediate banks to private investment, e.g. in Japan, South Korea, Taiwan and China

Slide 5 Three Different Financial-Industrial Systems

There are three major and different kinds of financial-industrial systems in the world. These are the Washington Consensus Neoclassical Zone, The Berlin Consensus Zone and the Tokyo Consensus Zone, as Slide 5 illustrates.

These different types or zones of financial-industrial systems produce radically different economic results (see note 6). The crucial difference between these three systems is the level of support given, or not given, to private investment in SMEs and large private companies by their systemically different behaviour.

The Washington Consensus Zone

1. **National governments borrow** to fund govt running costs
2. **Real indebtedness by governments** to third parties (lenders or banks)
3. **Government downsizing**
4. **Privatisation,** cuts in public services, economic stagnation and lower living standards
5. **Relatively few banks collect most saving**
6. **No investment credit banks**
7. **High interest cost margin** between CB cost of funds and market rates
8. No **government industrial policy**
9. **Low or absent growth reducing welfare, growing unemployment**
10. **Dominant neoclassical mindset by all active players**

Need for a rethink about all that - otherwise, continuing cultural decline

Slide 6 - the Washington Consensus Zone
Slide 6 lists the set of circumstances most of my listeners are familiar with - governments owing a lot to external lenders, who are being paid relatively high interest rates, government downsizing, privatisation, and cuts in public services with relative economic stagnation. And the financial accompaniment to that - a few major banks acting as drains to take away local saving, but not acting as taps for local SME investment, in countries that have no industrial policy.
In this zone there is a dominant neoclassical mindset by ALL players, all the political parties, all the media, virtually all the academic economists, nearly all the businessmen, and even most of the students of economics. Some of the media maintain a kind of

continual complaint about the destruction of the social fabric and increasing poverty due to government policies, but these media offer no practical alternative. There is a large and growing group of increasingly vociferous economics students who are "Rethinking Economics" because they are profoundly unhappy about the single mindset of their chosen subject.

The failure of the West is a cultural failure, brought about by a general belief in a neoclassical macroeconomics which does not produce the goods. This is the major reason why Shimomura was ignored - the West feels it already has all the answers.

That complacency is still a predominant attitude despite recent events.

The Berlin Consensus Zone

1. German domination of the EU
2. ECB follows Washington Consensus Zone policy except in Germany
3. Where the Sparkassen (local savings banks) collect a high percentage of local and national saving through 431 local banks with 15,600 branches and provide local taps for SME investment
4. Sparkassen are public banks committed to the alleviation of poverty and local economic success through the funding of SMEs

A   Local saving intermediated into local SME investment is the major factor in German economic success
B   There is No ECB foreign borrowing supporting the rescue of EU countries in difficulty - the support is ECB no-cost created fiat money

The Berlin Consensus Zone (Slide 7) is like the Washington Zone with one essential difference - in Germany there is a centuries-long tradition of hundreds of local public savings banks (currently 431) with thousands of branches (currently 15,600) collecting a large amount of national saving and lending it long-term to the SMEs in Germany's cities, towns and villages. Germany runs the EU because of its economic strength due to that Sparkassen system. The ECB does NOT borrow money to save the weaker EU economies - it's all created credit at the ECB.

Britain in 1800 resembled present-day Germany, with 800 local banks funding local industry in the early ferment of the industrial revolution.As Professor Glynn Davies told the Wilson Committee in 1979, if Britain had in the 18th century the financial system it had in the 1970s, the industrial revolution would have been stillborn.

The Tokyo (Shimomuran) Consensus Zone
(Japan, South Korea, Taiwan and China)

1. Purpose of financial system is funding investment
2. 10-20% of GDP pa is no-cost investment credit fiat-created by central banks
3. Credit source listed as "savings of the people" but the people have nothing to do with it
4. Loans and discounts to banks from CB have an interest rate = inflation rate of factory gate goods
5. That makes loan funds a counterpart of real resources
6. Earmarked credit for canalisation to private companies ("Convoy system" in Japan)
7. Tending to produce a continuous economic boom
8. Vast assets (of paper wealth) at the CB - interest-bearing loans repayable by the borrowing banks
9. ICC provides continuously rising government tax receipts

Or as Modern Monetary Theory puts it
"Government receives back in taxes part of the fiat created credit funded by its own IOUs"

Slide 8 - The Tokyo (Shimomuran) Consensus Zone
In the Tokyo Consensus Zone(see note 6) things are differently set up. The national financial systems are geared to funding private companies and for transmission of created credit from the Central Bank via local banks to local industries for the funding of high company liquidity, high levels of work in progress and finished goods, and new capital investment.

Investment credit creation occurs a high rate in the nation's central bank and that credit is "convoyed" (the Japanese money transmission system from the central bank to final users is called the "Convoy System") to private companies. The source of the created credit is listed as "The savings of the people" but that's not accurate - it's FIAT money, defined as freshly created credit which is money, because the govt says it is - and who has the power to disagree?

The setting of an basic interest rate which causes money to become the counterpart of real resources is the great stabiliser in the system.

The first Asian economic miracle was the Mantetsu. The first Western economic miracle was the USA from 1938-44 which grew at an unprecedented rate, as Slide 9 below illustrates.

Once upon a time in the USA - FDR's Economic Miracle 1938-44

1. **Financed by FED credit creation**
2. **(Allegedly financed by the "savings of the people")**
3. **Every investment required by the war effort funded either by investment credit or War Bonds**

Results

A.   **Economic growth averaged 12.2% for six years**
B.   **ICC created the USA as a hegemonic power**
C.   **Shimomura's late 1945 visit to the USA may have assisted the development of his economic understanding**

Slide 9 - Rapid US economic growth 1938-44

So investment credit creation, with its origin in the FED (the central bank of the USA) produced miraculous economic growth with limited inflation(see Note 7) (because John Kenneth Galbraith was running price controls).

No other wartime nation approached the economic growth rate of the USA. One economist certainly noticed that (see Slide 10 below for Alan Milward's Question).

Alan Milward's Question

"Granted that the United States had peculiar advantages in the quantity of resources, in freedom of intervention from the enemy, and in the great quantity of slack which existed in the economy before 1940, it remains a logical and revealing approach to ask precisely why the productive effort in other economies fell short of that in America."
Alan Milward, War Economy and Society 1939-45, Harmondsworth, Penguin, 1977, p75.

Slide 10 - Alan Milward's Question

On some UN estimates, the USA had about half the industrial power in the world by 1945, due to FDR's American Economic Miracle (1938-44): when FDR died on 12 April 1944 and Harry Truman became the 33rd US President, the miracle ended. Truman didn't like the idea of investment credit created debt for US businesses and SMEs. So the USA went back to much lower economic growth rates. In post war Japan circumstances were dire (see note 8). But as the old Greek idiom says, "Necessity is the mother of invention."

Japan's Post War Circumstances Were Dire

1. **About 40% of the urban area was destroyed in the 66 bombed cities**
2. **Over 600 major industrial facilities destroyed or badly damaged**
3. **Japanese wealth reduced by between a third and a quarter**
4. **Failure of the 1945 rice crop**
5. **2.5 million housing units destroyed, 8.5 million people homeless**
6. **About 760,000 SME premises destroyed**

Slide 11 - Japan's post war circumstances

Few countries have ever faced the degree of devastation which Japan's rulers did when the war ended.

The postwar Japanese Government was eventually forbidden to borrow (see Note 9) to restore their economy, as Dodge's (see note 10) 1948/9 advice required. But during the immediate post war period they wanted to rebuild their devastated infrastructure and restore their industries so they created credit to fund the private companies which could achieve their objectives.

Although the Dodge advice was finally written into law by the Japanese diet in 1948/49, it was followed in practice from 1945, and much of it was set out in the "Economic Stabilisation Program" of May 1947.

The Economic Context of Japanese Government Action

1 American Banker Joseph Morrel Dodge was advisor to the US Occupation Authorities
2 He recommended the Japanese Government should have a "balanced budget" that forbade Keynesian government borrowing
3 From Sept 1945 until 1964 the Japanese Government did not borrow at all

A BUT INSTEAD THEY CREATED FIAT INVESTMENT CREDIT AT THE BoJ
B TO REBUILD THEITR INFRASTRUCTURE AND RE_EQUIP THEIR INDUSTRIES

Slide 12 - The Economic Context of Japanese Government Action

In 1964 the Japanese Government did borrow for the first time - from the Japanese Post Office Savings Bank, which has provided since then total funds of between 6% to 10% of GDP to help counterbalance a little of the credit creation in Japan, investment credit credit which is currently running at about 226% of GDP in 2013.

Table 5.4. Credit Creation by the Japanese Banks.

Year	A Bank Advances (other than those by Bank of Japan) million yen	B Bank of Japan Loans and Discounts to the banking system million yen	$\frac{B}{A}$ =%	Bank of Japan Government bonds holdings million yen
1946 average	118,160	49,621	42	34,700
1947 ,,	136,843	43,906	32	145,800
1948 ,,	246,159	54,238	22	247,700
1949 ,,	494,431	77,792	16	188,600
1950 ,,	820,526	123,251	15	136,700
1951 ,,	1,241,180	179,502	14	126,000
1952 ,,	1,808,130	241,134	13	286,100
1953 ,,	2,391,795	307,490	13	314,300
1954 ,,	2,830,895	365,477	13	483,500
1955 end of year	3,195,800	319,000	10	553,600
1956 ,,	4,066,100	139,900	3	586,700
1957 ,,	5,024,400	551,900	11	387,200
1958 ,,	5,812,900	379,900	6·5	536,000
1959 ,,	6,802,800	337,900	5	644,800
1960 ,,	8,182,600	500,200	6	569,100
1961 ,,	9,770,100	1,284,500	13	287,700
1962 ,,	11,494,600	1,285,100	11	378,300
1963 ,,	14,562,600	1,155,600	8	346,000
1964 ,,	16,829,700	1,110,400	7	760,900
1965 ,,	19,217,900	1,627,700	8·5	930,000
1966 ,,	22,046,000	1,741,200	8	638,100
1967 ,,	25,323,000	1,515,100	6	1,144,000
1968 ,,	29,032,800	1,563,200	5	1,434,100

Sources : Japan Economic Yearbooks 1955, 1963, 1964-5, 1969.
  Statistics Department, The Bank of Japan, Hundred-Year Statistics of the Japanese Economy, 1966.
  Bureau of Statistics, Office of the Prime Minister, Monthly Statistics of Japan, May 1969.

Slide 13 *Credit Creation by the Bank of Japan* (source of table, Kenneth Bieda, *The Structure and Operation of the Japanese Economy,* John Wiley and Sons, Australasia PTY, 1970, p143.)

The extent of post-war Credit Creation by the Bank of Japan for Japanese Banks was very large, as Slide 13 shows.
Note that the BoJ purchase of bank bonds exceeded the bank advances in 1948. This is a very odd table - it calculates the percentage of end-year dependency rather than growth from the beginning of the year. The more usual growth formula is (B/A)/ (100-B/A) or 42/58 or 72% for 1946, and similarly 32/68 or 47% for 1947, and 22/78 or 28% in 1948, as shown on Slide 14 below.

Investment Credit Creation by the Japanese Banking System

Mid-Year	Increase in Bank Advances pa	Y/E Dependency on BoJ Loans	BOJ Loan Support
1946	72.3%	42%	72%
1947	15.8%	32%	47%
1948	79.9%	22%	28%
1949	100.9%	16%	19%
1950	66.0%	15%	18%
1951	51.3%	14%	16%
1952	45.7%	13%	15%

Source: Calculated from data on previous slide

Slide 14 - ICC growth in the Japanese Banking System

These vast increases in bank advances were one of the causes of the great Japanese infrastructure recovery with post-war inflation during 1945-49. A great many prewar bank loans were written off, mainly in 1947 and 1948, because the assets to which they related had been destroyed.

This created credit cost NOTHING to create. When some of that money was spent, the government received the "tax take" (then about 33% in Japan) as govt income.

So for every Y100 bn spent, the government received Y33 bn in return for no cost at all. Not surprisingly, Japan boomed. And as the years passed, the BoJ acquired vast assets in the form of Japanese Company interest-earning loans.

In order to be a banker, you have to be able "to tell a bill from a mortgage." The BoJ does not have loans owed to third parties - it has the rediscounted corporate loans of private companies, and these are interest earning assets. The CIA can't apparently make that distinction.

[See https://medium.com/@georgetaitedwards/the-public-debt-of-japan-and-china-e82292595d7a]

SME and Corporate Priorities in the Use Of Funds

1 Liquidity
2 Affordable work-in-progress and stock levels
3 Improve productivity with existing staff levels
4 Investment in plant and equipment

Slide 15- SME and Corporate Priorities in the use of funds

The data shows (see Slide 15 above and note 12) that a lot of the created funds remained in the bank accounts of borrowing companies to provide a cushion against hard times and to provide business confidence, which is the real root of high investment behaviour. High investment levels do not result from "animal spirits" (as some economic textbooks claim) but from high confidence based on much money in the bank. Liquidity is paramount over profitability, because low liquidity causes company bankruptcy while unprofitability is not immediately fatal. Profitable projects cannot be safely afforded unless there is no major risk to liquidity.

Credit creation funds long supply chains and high stock levels. The funding of work in progress and finished goods is usually the second priority of goods producing companies. Stock levels are abnormally high in all investment credit economies because that's affordable - high levels of credit removes the over-trading route to bankruptcy. The greatest productivity gains within investment credit economies does not arise from the employment of staff in new enterprises but from the productivity increases widely available when existing company staff use updated equipment. Of course investment in up to date plant and equipment in new companies has the highest return but is not so frequently encountered as the upskilling of existing staff using new machinery.

During the 1945-72 period the observed levels of company funds in the nation's banks as a percentage of GDP have tended to be about 30% in Japan, about 15% in Germany and about 7% in the UK. Because high levels of liquidity produce business confidence and high investment, investment was highest in Japan, middling in Germany and low in the UK (see note 13).

During the late 1960s and 1970s, the Japanese car showrooms, providing cars manufactured thousands of miles away, were better stocked and with much shorter delivery times than locally built UK cars.

The Japanese post-war government from 1945 to 1951 saw major annual increases in its income because the created credit generated subsequent tax revenues (then running at c33% of total private expenditure) for government. There is no better illustration of the basic truth of Modern Monetary Theory, of a government creating vast flows of "Fiat money" by making an IOU to itself, and then receiving through the tax take about 33% of that IOU back in the form of taxes paid on the expenditure of that money.

The picture of postwar Japan illustrated by these slides is quite amazing. Japan had lost a lot of its infrastructure, industry and housing through bombing, yet a couple or three years after the war ended, rich industries with 30% of GDP in the bank were confidently re-employing people to rebuild their infrastructures and re-equip their industries using the skills of their people and management organisational skills - and their Government's understanding of investment credit economics - to restore their economy.

Major Changes of Focus in BoJ Credit Creation

Era	Primary Policy Focus	Secondary Policy Focus
1945-51	Fixing war damage	Raising Government Income
1952-59	Private industrial investment	Creating trading advantage
1960-68	Doubling living stadards	Improving social benefits
1989-85	Increasing trading advantage	Increasing Japan's status
1986-91	Funding asset bubble	Power redistribution
1991-2010	BoJ independence	Structural change
2011-15	21st century Abenomics	Re-establishing Shim'n economy

Slide 16 - Major eras in BoJ Credit Creation

The focus of Bank of Japan Credit Creation continually changed throughout the 1945-2015 period. Once the infrastructure and SME production had been restored, the focus shifted to the creation of large investments in heavy industry - e.g. in metal processing and production plants, in order to enable the inputs to motor vehicle and shipping industries. The earlier post-war focus had re-established Japan's millions of SMEs as a domestic source of products and services and the 1951 change in focus away from SME credit availability led to the bankruptcy of some SMEs. The Japanese Finance Minister, then Hiyato Ikeda, had to resign in 1952 after commenting in the Japanese diet that "it makes no difference to me if five or ten small businessmen are forced to commit suicide." (see note13).

During the early 1960s, the Japanese Ikeda administration stated its priority was the doubling of Japanese living standards over a ten-year period. The acknowledged major author of that "income-doubling plan" was Dr Osamu Shimomura (See note 14) That objective was achieved three years early in 1967, along with major improvements in the Japanese social package (statutory minimum wage legislation in 1959, a universal national pension and health insurance in 1961, and various measures for the better care for the aged in the Welfare Law of 1963). Paper wealth and economic wealth is created if the loans result in investments that produce real wealth and are repaid out of genuine growth.

**The Five Major Forms of Credit Creation
Inherent in the Work of the Three Master Economists
JM Keynes, Dr Osamu Shimomura and Professor Richard Werner**

1. **Credit Creation for Consumers -** Keynesian remedy for deficient demand
2. **Investment Credit Creation -** Shimomuran-Wernerian remedy for deficient supply - productive ICC supply-side economics - see "new paradigm in macroeconomics" by Professor Richard Werner
3. **Financial Credit Creation -** to stabilise a banking system and guarantee its liquidity
4. **Speculative Credit Creation -** to fund an "unintended" asset bubble e.g. in Japan 1986-91- see Richard Werner's book "Princes of the Yen"
5. **Invention and Innovation Credit Creation -** to fund rapid scientific advance and innovations in manufacturing

Slide 17 The Five Major Forms of Credit Creation

This slide puts the five different forms of credit creation and their associated master economists into context. Many people have the simple belief that all debt is bad, but life is much too complicated for that to be valid. Many Western economists are in the mental prison created by neoclassical economics. My comments on each kind of credit creation are:

1 Credit Creation for Consumers First, if an economy has deficient demand, creating credit for consumers is the right Keynesian and government response. The trouble with the 1970s in the UK was that credit was created to increase demand when local supply was insufficient, so inflation and higher imports resulted. Nowadays there are trillions of ECB euros which were created to support Greek, Spanish, and other unbalanced budgets. ECD loan support has only preserved their existing national state of poverty without increasing prosperity, and unless the EU brightens up, Greece may leave the union.
2 Investment Credit Creation for private industry provides a Shimomuran- Wernerian economics of effective supply, for rapid wealth creation via long term low-repayment cost loans to millions

of SMEs and private companies for increased liquidity, more affordable WIP and productivity-increasing investments. See Richard Werner's book "new paradigm in economics".

3 Financial Credit Creation - eg £375n of BoE UK Clearing Bank Support. FCC stabilises the banking system but doesn't do anything else. A banking system is vital in all countries, but what's the point of stabilising a banking system without making due provision for the investment credit which produces prosperity?

4 Speculative Credit Creation is what independent Central Banks tend to do - e.g. in Japan 1986-91 - again, see Werner's books "Princes of the The Yen" and "new paradigm in economics". Speculation - gambling with bank funds - is the fastest way for bankers to get big bonuses, and legislation is needed to ensure banks operate within prudential rules according to their function, or recurrent crises are inevitable. Credit should never be created for this purpose.

5 Invention and innovation Credit Creation - eg FDR and the $2bn to develop and build atomic bombs, FDR's WWII 50 Synthetic Rubber Factories, Kennedy's Moonshot programme, Obama's Energy Self-Sufficiency Initiative and Green Energy Development, Silicon Valley and the Apple inventions etc

Finally, neoclassical economics is the destruction of credit and the opposite of all these above.

The Key Shimomuran Amendment to Keynes' Saving-Investment Equation

Shimomura replaces the Keynesian saving-investment equilibrium condition with the equation

$$S+D = Is + Id$$

That is, Saving (S) plus Debt (D, equal to investment credits arising from investment credit creation at the Bank of Japan) equals Is (Investment financed by saving) plus Id (Investment financed by debt)

Slide 18 - The Key Shimomuran Amendment to Keynes' Savings-Investment Equilibrium

This key equation (see notes 15,16) means that the investment level of Japan is increased by credit creation with its initial impetus in the Central Bank of Japan. This equation replaces the classic Keynesian Savings-Investment equality with a much more useful formula because the government of a country can increase the nation's investment level (and hence its future growth and prosperity) through government policy to produce earmarked investment credit creation at the Central Bank. The model suggests an increase in the investment level of about 15% of GDP a year is available. This is Shimomura's key amendment to macroeconomic theory.

What did Shimomura do in his economic model of Japan?

1. He took three of John Maynard Keynes' observations and restructured these into a fresh economic understanding, a new Harrod-Domar model of the Japanese economy.
2. He eventually (in early 1961) presented that Model of the Japanese Economy and its equations to the joint meeting of the Japanese Economic Association and the Japanese Econometric Society.
3. His presentation was then published under the title "Seicho Seisaku No Kihon Mondai" (Basic Problems of Growth Policy) in Riron Keizaigaku, March 1961.

Slide 19 - What Shimomura did

Shimomura used his insights to practical effect for many years before he published his "Economic Model of Japan".
Keynes 'three observations" are
1 - there is no intrinsic reason for the shortage of capital; therefore
2 -savings can be created (and investments made) prior of the returns which justify them; and
3 - government can appear to "pay" for that credit creation by taking out a charge (or IOU) against itself (a point which resides at the heart of Modern Monetary Theory).(see note 17)

"If, therefore, greater investment can be financed partly by credits, there is no need for that 'abstinence' which the classical economists considered necessary for economic progress, any more than there is for that 'austerity' which some present day underdeveloped countries impose on already under-consuming populations at the constant peril of social unrest. Nor is it difficult, in such credit-creating circumstances, to agree with Keynes' observation that investment and consumption should be regarded as complementary rather than competitive."

(Kenneth K. Kurihara, *The Growth Potential of the Japanese Economy,* Baltimore, John Hopkins Press 1971 page 138)Slide 21 - Kurihara's towering conclusion

Slide 20 - Professor Kenneth K Kurihara's Conclusion

The Japanese-born American-educated Professor Kenneth Kenkichi Kurihara (1910-1972) (see note 18) was an acknowledged expert in growth economics. The insights in Kurihara's greatest book "The Growth Potential of the Japanese Economy" (John Hopkins Press Maryland 1971) should have been integrated into Western macro-economic theory by now. His book is the best English language window into Shimomuran economics, with 47 references to Dr Osamu Shimomura. As Slide 21 says "Greater investment financed partly by credits" - now there's the solution to the West's current economic difficulties, and the EU and the USA need to learn and adopt Shimomuran economics asap. "No need for abstinence "- now that will be news to the currently suffering Greeks, Italians, Spanish and French! "No need for austerity" - well, that again will certainly be news to the IMF, the ECB, the World Bank, and the British Treasury.
And investment and consumption are complementary, therefore there is no need to cut consumption to fund investment. Investment Credit Economics seems to have been independently invented twice - In South Manchuria and in the USA - and copied three times, in South Korea, Taiwan and China (in historical order). (The"Manchurians" or Japanese leaders of the South Manchuria Railway Co at first developed Manchuria then relocated to Japan where they used the same understanding and processes to restore Japan's fortunes.)

None of these are minor matters. See Note 19 for a reference to nine articles written by Bryan Gould and me on how the UK could flourish using Shimomuran economics.

Shimomuran Economics
Will Ultimately Triumph in the West because it

1. Re-establishes government as the main enabler of wealth creation and assists the continuation of political unions (eg, the EU, the UK)
2. Does not require a revolution in income distribution - it permits the rich to keep what they have while enabling government to act in the interests of all their people - that's a great advantage to everybody
3. More fully enables local saving to fund the conversion of local invention to local production - cf Schumpeter
4. Accelerates the adoption of more expensive greener technologies
5. Reduces income differentials by involving everyone in the economic growth process
6. Offers a better path to prosperity to than any other macroeconomic understanding

Slide 21 - The Ultimate Triumph of Sihmomuran-Wernerian Economics

To take each point in turn:

1 Shimomuran-Wernerian economics is a wealth creating macroeconomics

2 This macroeconomics doesn't need any kind of revolution, because it works well without one

3 Previously, the West invents and the East invests - but understanding this system permits production to be created nearer to the point of invention

4 It makes more expensive greener technologies affordable e.g. sea-based windfarms, German state-of-the-art modern coal fired power stations with the shutdown of the out of date UK equivalent, etc, etc

5 It reduces income differentials and improves median incomes by funding local innovation and

6 It's the best available macroeconomic option, but Western politicians, business men and women, economists and the media need to understand it in detail soon.

My Conclusions

1. Shimomuran-Wernerian macroeconomics is the key to higher growth and the major path to prosperity for all economies
2. There is a timely of up to 80 years in the spread of economic understanding and practice
3. Long-term Investment Credit Debt is good for SMEs and all public and private companies but it is not a panacea
4. A "world of abundant capital" is made possible by Shimomuran-Wernerian macroeconomics - not a nation or a region but a world
5. Shimomuran-Wernerian macroeconomics may be Modern Monetary Theory in its greatest form - the creation of fiat credit for canalisation to SMEs and larger local private enterprises for the continual conversion of invention to innovation to bring about widely-shared continually higher standards in a greener high technology world
6. "Mea Culpa"

Slide 22 - My Conclusions

Again, by each point:

1.This fresh-to-the-West economics is the major path to widespread prosperity for everybody. A sound macroeconomic understanding is the precondition for wealth creation.
2. One major wrong assumption in neo-classical economics is that everybody in the world has access to the same technology (when they don't) and that new understandings spread instantaneously (when they don't) especially not in economics.(see note 20).
3. Debt has been demonised in the West, but the right kind of debt is the path to prosperity. Investment credit creation can increase investment and growth, enabling the "rest to catch up with the West" (cf the works of Alice Amsden) and requiring the West to become better, even in economic understanding.(see Note 21). But it is neither a free lunch for borrowing companies nor a panacea!
4. Shinzo Abe, who I am delighted to note has recently won another election, spoke to the Japanese Press Club on 19 April 2013 about his "new" Shimomuran policies and spoke of a "Japan of Abundant Capital" based on no-cost investment credit creation. But this new economics is not just for abundant capital in a nation like Japan or

for a region (like the Tokyo Consensus group) - it's for the better development of the whole world.

5. This economics is based on some of the insights of Keynes (but available though the deep reading of his original works, not as most know him, through his interpreters) and is consistent with MMT. It puts productive power behind the limitless ingenuity of mankind and validates Schumpeter's key insight that the innovator is the crucial player in the economic development process. Professor Richard Werner was the first 1991 Shimomura fellow, but the Development Bank of Japan told Werner nothing about Shimomura, yet Richard has reverse-engineered much of Shimomuran macroeconomics economics from Japan's financial statistics, using the relatively new technology of Granger Predictive Analysis - a very impressive feat.

6. Finally, thank you for your attention to this lecture. I know my omissions about this new economics are much greater than my inclusions. Shimomuran economics is a large and complex macroeconomic system, not just a few key observations, and there is an entire raft of the machinery of government, a complex set of policies, and feedback monitoring which are indispensable parts of making this better macroeconomics work well, as well as methods for the control of inflation and a set of preconditions including Central Bank subsidiarity, and these of abundant capital to accelerate the greening of all economic activities which I have not covered - but I do hope I have said enough to let you see the possibility of a newer, lovelier world of abundant capital, where poverty can really be made history and where the boundless ingenuity of mankind and womankind can flourish to bring about a much more satisfactory and sustainable world for all of us. And so be it, preferably soon (see note 22). Last year I wrote two books on this subject. The first is mainly a book of collected essays and the second is the "Story of the economic bomb" and the book covers in grayscale look like this:

Slide 23 - The Front Covers in grayscale of two of my books

These two 2014 books by the author are "Shimomuran Economics and the Rise of the Tokyo Consensus" at http://www.lulu.com/shop/george-tait-edwards/shimomuran-economics/paperback/product-21688864.html and "Lucky Bastards of the 20th Century - The Story of the EconomicBomb" which is showcased at https://medium.com/@georgetaitedwards/lucky-bastards-of- the-20th-century-8bd352881b6b and available at http:// www.lulu.com/shop/george-tait-edwards/ lucky-bastards-of- the-20th-century/paperback/product-21913362.html

Notes to the Gresham College lecture

Note 1: In my opinion Dr Osamu Shimomura was the greatest economist of the 20th century after John Maynard Keynes. See https://medium.com/@georgetaitedwards/the-master-economist-2a744a336ece.

Note 2: Many of the facts and comments about Doctor Osamu Shimomura's life are at the Development Bank of Japan Website at http://www.dbj.jp/ricf/en/fellowship/ (where a fellowship is offered in Shimomura's memory). For a more full consideration of Dr Osamu Shimomura's life, see Part 2 of "Shimomuran Economics and the Rise of the Tokyo Consensus" at http://www.lulu.com/ shop/ george-tait-edwards/shimomuran-economics/paperback/ product-21715259.html

Note 3: As part of Treaty of Portsmouth, Russia was required (among other things) to return its leases in southern Manchuria (containing Port Arthur and Talien) to China, and to turn over the South Manchurian Railway and its mining concessions to Japan. The Mantetsu company was funded by BoJ debt, and made most of its money by growing and transporting soya beans, and the area of the Mantetsu became a highly developed and prosperous quasi-independent colony with much higher living standards than those in Japan at that time. See http://en.wikipedia.org/wiki/ South_Manchuria_Railway.

Note 4 The summary of the book "The Comprehensive History of the South Manchurian Railway " says:

"The 40-year history of the Mantetsu fascinates not only Japanese historians but also the general public, partly because of the image that Japanese were building a new semi- autonomous state outside of Japan. More than 1 million Japanese civilians migrated to Manchuria to begin a new life in better economic conditions. They had a western colonial lifestyle, enjoying golf clubs, large parks, and western style housing. The special express trains called "Asia" were among the fastest, best appointed trains in the world. The capital of Manchukuo [満州国], Hsinching [新京 - literally "New Capital"] (now Changchun [长长春]), was built with modern urban planning with avenues and streets akin to Paris. In 1937, the Mantetsu owned 15 companies, 32 subsidiary companies, and invested in 33 more companies. They operated transport (rails, shipping, and airline), industry (steel mill, chemical, oil refinery, cement, textile, sugar), commerce (trading, retail), construction, lumber, minerals (coal and gold), electric and gas power, real estate, telecommunication and the press, and hotel chains. By its end, the Mantetsu ran or owned 71 companies with 340,000 employees, including 248,000 Chinese and Russians." See http://www.japansociety.org.uk/20591/the-comprehensive-history-of-south-manchurian-railways-company-%E6%BA%80%E9%89%84%E5%85%A8%E5%8F%B2/

Note 5 Shinzo Abe's grandfather was Nobusuke Kishi, who was Japan's postwar Prime Minster as well as one of the leaders ("the chief industrial planner") of the development of the South Manchurian Railway Company during the 1930s. See http://vitaleevan.org/2014/12/12/for-japans-shinzo-abe-unfinished-family-business-wall-street- journal/ and http://du.w2ex.me/page/8/

Note 6 See https://medium.com/@georgetaitedwards/a-comparison-of-the-washington-berlin-and-tokyo-consensus-zones-221e7e53018b

Note 7 See http://londonprogressivejournal.com/article/view/1507/fdrs-american-economic-miracle-or-the-first-economic-bomb-the-usa-from-to-part For a definition and explanation of credit creation see the "Appendix: A Note on Credit Creation" at pages 179-181 of "Reversing Economic Decline", John C.Carrington and George T. Edwards, Macmillan, London 1981.

Note 8 See http://en.wikipedia.org/wiki/Air_raids_on_Japan

Note 9 For other comments on Japan's economic miracle, see http://londonprogressivejournal.com/article/view/1566/the-origin-of-shimomuras-japanese-economic- miracle-or-the-second-economic-bomb-japan-from-to-economic-miracles-part

Note 10 Some commentary about Joseph Dodge's role in Japan's post war economic policy is at https://books.google.co.uk/books?id=_b7KTEkuDSUC&pg=PA48&lpg=PA48&dq=joseph+dodge+japan&source=bl&ots=QgJVc2n2Rd&sig=_2MZ2n4KsHfSMcRjX1PwuaufnaQ&hl=en&sa=X&ei=DprQVLGrFJLSaMC0gZgN&ved=0CE4Q6AEwCw#v=onepage&q=joseph%20dodge %20japan&f=false

Note 11 As Kenneth Bieda calculates on p 143 of "The Structure and Operation of the Japanese Economy,"John Wiley and Sons, Australia

Pty, in his Table 5.4 "Credit Creation by the Japanese Banks", the extent of the overloan (or the Bank of Japan loan and discounts to the Banking System) was 42% in 1946, 32% in 1947, 22% in 1948, and 16% in 1949. The 1946/47 growth in the overloan as a percentage of the original start-of-year net loanable bank funds (assuming no credit creation in the banking system) would have been 42/(100-42) or 42/5811 or 72.4%. That is, the BoJ loans to the banking system during the year were 72.4% of the original funds, and 42% of the total funds in the system at the year-end. No nation has ever saved 72.4% of the loanable funds in its banking system in any year - the only possible source of these funds is created credit at the BoJ. In the devastated war-damaged economy of 1946 Japan, the "people" could not possibly save 72.4% of the loanable bank funds during the first post-war year. And even if by some miracle they had, could they possibly "save" 47% of these expanded funds in previous year bank deposits in the following year of 1947, 28% in 1948 and 19% in 1949? The average compound annual growth rate in total Japanese bank loans was 39.6% per annum from the beginning of 1945 until the end of 1951, when total bank loan funds were 5.29 times the original funds. The only source of that great financial asset growth was BoJ credit creation.

Note 12 See p110-17 of "Lucky Bastards of the 20th Century - The Story of the Economic Bomb", George Tait Edwards, showcased at https://medium.com/@georgetaitedwards/ lucky-bastards-of-the-20th-century-8bd352881b6b and available for purchase at http://www.lulu.com/shop/george-tait-edwards/lucky-bastards-of-the-20th-century/paperback/ product-21958236.html

Note 13 See the Wikipedia entry about Hayato Ikeda at http://en.wikipedia.org/wiki/Hayato_Ikeda

Note 14 See the extensive commentary about Shimomura's contribution to Japanese economic thinking and the income-doubling plan at pages 99-105 of "Comparing Post War Japanese and Finnish Economies and Societies"edited by Yashusi Tanaka, Toshiaki Amika, Jan Ojala and Jari Eleranta on the internet at https://books.google.co.uk/books?id=sT5WBQAAQBAJ&pg=PA101&lpg=PA101&dq=Osamu+Shimomura+economist+1910-89&source=bl&ots=g9uv_HoqGG&sig=g5OhiZlWGSRgji25zXyr3cJX5GU&hl=en&sa=X&ei=tn3eVO7VA8XxULevhOAI&ved=0CD4Q6AEwBQ#v=onepage&q=

Osamu%20Shimomura_%20economist%201910-89&f=false
Note 15 See https://medium.com/@georgetaitedwards/the-master-economist-2a744a336ece and for for the location of some of Shimomura's works in Western libraries, see https:// medium.com/ @georgetaitedwards/there-are-now-three-books-by-dr-osamu-shimomura-1910-1989-in-the-national-library-of-e4f34c351402 and https://medium.com/ @georgetaitedwards/the-british-library-now-have-five-works-by-the-master-economist-dr-osamu-shimomura-1910-1989-c9c4b6df6af. The Library of Congress have eleven of Dr Osamu Shimomura's works - more than those in any other Western library - but due to the dominance of the neoclassical mindset in the USA, these books have not conferred any advantage upon American economic understanding. See https://medium.com/ @georgetaitedwards/us-sources-for- several-of-the-works-of-dr-osamu-shimomura-1910-1989-eleven-in-the-library-91f4b75290d0. According to the Development Bank of Japan, Shimomura's Major Works are

1. Keizai hendō no jōsū bunseki 経済変動の乗数分析,1952 (Economic Fluctuation and Multiplier Analysis)2.Keizai seichō jitsugen no tame ni 経済成長長実現のために, 1958 (Achieving Economic Growth) 3.Nihon keizai seichōron 日日本経済成長長論, 1962
(A Theory of Japanese Economic Growth)

4.Nihon keizai wa seichō suru 日日本経済は成長長する, 1963
(The Japanese Economy Will Grow)

5.Keizaitaikoku Nihon no sentaku 経済大大国日日本の選択, 1971
(Japan's Choices as a Major Economic Power)

6.Zero seichō dasshutsu no jōken ゼロ成長長脱出の条件, 1976
(Conditions for Escaping from [Japanese] Zero Growth)

7.Nihon keizai no setsudo 日日本経済の節度, 1981
(Discipline and the Japanese Economy)

8.Nihon wa warukunai 日日本は悪くない, 1987(Japan Is Not at Fault)
See http://www.dbj.jp/ricf/en/fellowship/.
Note 17 Again, see https://medium.com/@georgetaitedwards/the-master- economist-2a744a336ece
Note 18 See "The Key Relevance of the Writings of Professor

Kenneth Kenkichi Kurihara" at http://
londonprogressivejournal.com/article/view/1565/the-key-relevance-
of-the-writings-of-professor- Kenneth-Kenkichi-Kurihara
Note 19 See Bryan Gould and George Tait Edwards, Policies for an
Incoming Labour Government, published at http://
londonprogressivejournal.com/article/view/2122
Note 20 "See "How long will the West lag behind Asian Economic
Understanding?" at https:// medium.com/@georgetaitedwards/how-
long-will-the-west-lag-behind-23df18600dab
Note 21 For an article about the many possibilities made available by
investment credit economics, see http://
londonprogressivejournal.com/article/view/1685/the-many-major-
uses-of- investment-credit-creation-a-brief-walk-through-the-
observed-results-so-far-and-the-future- possibilities-made-available-
through-shimomuran-economics
Note 22 See https://medium.com/@georgetaitedwards/the-rough-
guide-to-shimomuran- economics-e9dca42c6808.

For further reading, see http://londonprogressivejournal.com/user/
view/2285 and https:// medium.com/@georgetaitedwards/the-rough-
guide-to-shimomuran-economics-e9dca42c6808 and two 2014 books
by the author at "Shimomuran Economics and the Rise of the Tokyo
Consensus" at http://www.lulu.com/shop/george-tait-edwards/
shimomuran-economics/paperback/ product-21688864.html and
"Lucky Bastards of the 20th Century - The Story of the Economic
Bomb" which is showcased at https://medium.com/
@georgetaitedwards/lucky-bastards-of-
the-20th-century-8bd352881b6b and available at http://
www.lulu.com/shop/george-tait-edwards/ lucky-bastards-of-the-20th-
century/paperback/product-21913362.html

To find many more works, search for Shimomuran Economics or my
full name on the internet, or refer to the listings at Appendix 2.

4.10 26th March 2015 "How Japan Zoomed from War Devastation into Prosperity 1945-52"

The following article was first produced on March 26 2015 at https://medium.com/@georgetaitedwards/how-japan-zoomed-from-war-devastation-into-prosperity-1945-52-92cad27eea81

The most astonishing economic recovery in the world is the story of how the Japanese created an economic explosion based and founded upon the ruins of the Second World War, the skills of the Japanese people and the economic understanding of the Japanese Government. It is an object lesson for the impoverished nations of the third world as well as for the United Kingdom and Greece. This is how it happened:

"1 Introduction
At the end of the Second World War, Japan had been utterly devastated. It had been a nation which had never lost a war and hence had never been occupied. No Japanese person prior to 1945 could possibly have imagined the disastrous circumstances which made an unconditional surrender inevitable.

2 Japanese Post-War Circumstances
A short and limited list of these most terrible circumstances were

- millions of Japanese had been killed and about 40% of the urban area destroyed in the 66 bombed cities
- over 600 major industrial facilities were destroyed or had sustained major damage
- Japanese wealth had been reduced by between a quarter and a third
- the 1945 rice crop had failed
- 2.5 million houses had been destroyed, with 8.5 million homeless people
- about 760,000 SME premises had been destroyed, and
- Hiroshima and Nagasaki had been devastated by atomic bombs.

The effects of nearly all of the quantified factors listed above have been understated for political reasons. During the immediate post war period, the Japanese authorities wanted to pretend that they had been able to prevent US bombing when they had not and could not, and the US Occupation Authority forces wanted to pretend, for postwar reconciliation purposes, that the bombing had been less destructive of lives and properties than it had been.

3 The Japanese "Manchurians"

And with the end of the war, the million or so Japanese who had emigrated to the colony of Manchuria returned to Japan. The South Manchurian Railway Company—The Mantetsu—was the first high-growth investment credit economy in the world, which during the 1930s contributed about 25% to the income of the Japanese Government. The Japanese who had managed that first 20th century economic miracle, were repatriated with the practical knowledge of the high-growth economic technology which they promptly transplanted to Japanese soil. These new economic managers of Japan, who were referred to by the Japanese as "the Manchurians" (initially perhaps as an insult but ultimately with some awe) introduced in Japan everything they had learned about economic growth acceleration in Manchuria.

The Manchurian economic miracle had been almost wholly funded by fiat money—no-cost Bank of Japan created credit. The "Manchurians" promptly arranged that the BoJ created vast flows of no-cost investment credit to enable the funding of private industry to restore the infrastructure of Japan. The enormous scale of these credit-created funds (which, I repeat, cost nothing to create) is illustrated in Table 1 below. The bank advances to non-financial companies of 118.16 billion yen which kick-started the Japanese economy in 1946 were 31.1% of Japan's GDP of 378.9 billion yen that year, and a similar calculation for 1947 and 1948 shows bank advances were 12.1% and 11.4% of GDP during these two following years.

4 Credit Creation in the Japanese Economy

The investment credit creation in post war Japan was at first matched with Keynesian demand management—printing credit for consumption—and inflation soared. There were initially six key shortages in the rebirth of Japan's industrial economy—these were inadequate supplies of food, steel, cement, machinery, raw materials and energy. The Japanese Government established the1946 Food Control Law but the rations based upon the officially available supplies of food were inadequate to sustain life. As Kenichi Ohno reported in The Economic Development of Japan, Grips Development Forum, p146–7

"It is reported that Judge Yoshitada Yamaguchi of Tokyo District Court was so honest that he did not want to break the Food Control Law. He ate only rationed food and refused to take advantage of illegal food. In October 1947, he died of starvation."

A massive informal market, based on bartering goods for food, immediately sprung up when the war ended to supply some of the food to which the official agencies had no access. The morning trains from Tokyo to the surrounding areas—sometimes called the "onion trains"—were full of food-seeking commuters carrying kimonos and small goods to barter for food from the surrounding farms.That barter-based informal market fed the population of Tokyo until American food aid came through in late 1946 and 1947. During 1945 and 1946 many previous Japanese city dwellers relocated to the countryside to work in the farms for food. That situation (most obvious in Tokyo) happened in all the Japanese cities.

It is difficult and nearly impossible to study post-war Japanese food supplies in any great depth because the required data about the informal market does not exist except in a theoretical ("this must have happened, because the people survived") format.
Part of what had been experienced in Manchuria—high inflation in steel prices—was once again initially encountered in Japan. Without steel, larger buildings cannot be safely and cheaply constructed, and without cement the essential infrastructure of a modern economy—its public buildings, roads, ports and airfields—cannot be rebuilt. Without machinery the productivity of the people cannot flourish: without raw materials, industry cannot produce finished goods;

without energy the wheels of industry and transport cannot turn. Because 80% of Japanese shipping had been destroyed during the war, imports of food and energy (coal and oil) and raw materials depended on the grace and favour of the US Occupation Authorities, who enabled these imports to assist Japanese recovery.

But the Japanese had two tremendous advantages—first, a government which, through its employment of the "Manchurians" understood how to create high economic growth, and second, a highly educated and practical workforce who either possessed the required skills to run modern industries, or who could rapidly learn these skills where they did not previously exist.

Table 1: Credit Creation by the Japanese Banks

Table 5.4. Credit Creation by the Japanese Banks.

Year	A Bank Advances (other than those by Bank of Japan) million yen	B Bank of Japan Loans and Discounts to the banking system million yen	$\frac{B}{A}$ =%	Bank of Japan Government bonds holdings million yen
1946 average	118,160	49,621	42	34,700
1947 „	136,843	43,906	32	145,800
1948 „	246,159	54,238	22	247,700
1949 „	494,431	77,792	16	188,600
1950 „	820,526	123,251	15	136,700
1951 „	1,241,180	179,502	14	126,000
1952 „	1,808,130	241,134	13	286,100
1953 „	2,391,795	307,490	13	314,300
1954 „	2,830,895	365,477	13	483,500
1955 end of year	3,195,800	319,000	10	553,600
1956 „	4,066,100	130,000	3	500,700
1957 „	5,024,400	551,900	11	387,200
1958 „	5,812,900	379,900	6·5	536,000
1959 „	6,802,800	337,900	5	644,800
1960 „	8,182,600	500,200	6	569,100
1961 „	9,770,100	1,284,500	13	287,700
1962 „	11,494,600	1,285,100	11	378,300
1963 „	14,562,600	1,155,600	8	346,000
1964 „	16,829,700	1,110,400	7	760,900
1965 „	19,217,900	1,627,700	8·5	930,000
1966 „	22,046,000	1,741,200	8	638,100
1967 „	25,323,000	1,515,100	6	1,144,000
1968 „	29,032,800	1,563,200	5	1,434,100

Sources: *Japan Economic Yearbooks* 1955, 1963, 1964-5, 1969.
Statistics Department, The Bank of Japan, *Hundred-Year Statistics of the Japanese Economy*, 1966.
Bureau of Statistics, Office of the Prime Minister, *Monthly Statistics of Japan*, May 1969.

5 Economic Growth in Post War Japan,1946–52

Japanese bank advances had grown by a factor of 15.2, from 118.2 billion yen in 1946 to 1.808 trillion yen in 1952, at an average compound annual rate of 57.4% a year (see reference to Table 1 above). During the same period, the compound annual average rate of Japanese economic growth was 10.4% pa (see Table2).The "Manchurians" clearly knew what they were doing. They had prioritised recovery and growth over inflation. The achievement of a completely restored economy within half a dozen years was an amazing achievement by any criterion. Many Western observers, visiting Japan in the 1947–49 years, could not believe their eyes. The restoration of Japanese cities and facilities was so great that these observers felt obliged to argue that the wartime destruction of Japanese facilities must have been less than the US had claimed, because in their opinion, no nation could possibly have recovered that quickly. But the photographs of the widespread wartime destruction cannot be denied; the data about the devastation had been understated, not overestimated, and the reality was a greater devastation than had been recorded: and the economic recovery of fixed assets was as real as the destruction had been. Many Keynesian-trained economists saw the high rate of Japanese economic growth as due to the US contracts for military supplies for the Korean War (25 June 1950–27 July 1953). [We now know that was a 1% explanation.] But these contracts could only be placed because Japan had the facilities in place to supply these munitions. The economic miracle of Japan from 1945–52 (and, come to that, from 1945–74) was a supply side miracle, a miracle of the recreation of ALL of the facilities of a modern economy, not just these facilities the USA found convenient to use when the Korean War occurred.

Table 2 Rate of Japanese Real GDP Growth

Year	Yen Bn	Economic growth rate
1946	111 492	8.65%
1947	120 377	7.96%
1948	138 290	14.88%
1949	147 534	6.68%
1950	160 966	9.10%
1951	181 025	12.46%
1952	202 005	11.58%

Source: Japanese Real GDP Growth, 1925–2001

See http://socialdemocracy21stcentury.blogspot.co.uk/2013/01/ japanese-real-gdp-growth-19252001.html [a very good source website for this kind of data]

Furthermore, the US occupation had an American Banker by the name of Joseph Morrell Dodge as an advisor to the occupation authorities, and he recommended that the Japanese Government should have a "balanced budget". So from 1949 there was no Keynesian borrowing to fund recovery (and as an act of policy, the Japanese government did not borrow but created no-cost investment credit anyway). From September 1949 until 1964 the Japanese Government could not legally borrow at all either at home or abroad. They just created BoJ investment credit to provide the liquidity, the working capital and the investment capital required to rebuild their industries with up to date equipment. That procedure cost nothing and conferred great economic benefits.

The Japanese post-war government from 1945 to 1951 saw major annual increases in its income because the created credit generated subsequent tax revenues (then running at c33% of total private expenditure) for government. There is no better illustration of the basic truth of Modern Monetary Theory, of a government creating vast flows of "Fiat money" by making an IOU to itself, and then receiving through the tax take, about 33% of that IOU back in the form of taxes paid on the expenditure of that money.

6 Conclusions

The picture of postwar Japan illustrated by the above data is quite amazing. Japan had lost a great deal of its infrastructure, industry and housing through bombing. 80% of its shipping had been lost, and about 25% to 33% of its previous asset wealth. Yet in a couple or three years after the war ended, rich industries with 30% of GDP in the bank were confidently re-employing people to rebuild Japan's infrastructures and re-equip its industries using the skills of the people and management organisational skills—and their Government's understanding of investment credit economics—to restore the economy.

Professor Richard Werner's observations on these events—that it took only a year from 1945 and wartime destruction to the establishment of rapid economic development in Japan via investment credit economics, but after more than twenty years of neoclassical economics in Japan from 1991, Japan has still not recovered—are entirely relevant.

And Western economists should note that the Japanese economic miracle did not start in the 1960s when the West was first affected by it, because Western industries only came under competitive attack then. One question from the audience during the Gresham College Conference (referenced below) suggested that the economic recovery of Japan was just a post-war phenomenon. But rapid Japanese economic development continued for nearly three decades. High rates of Japanese economic growth began in the post war period and continued in an unbroken line from 1945 until at least 1974 when the high price of oil shocked Japan into a lower growth rate.

And it was a superior economic understanding—Shimomuran-Wernerian investment credit macroeconomics, named for the two master economists who have explained it—which produced that explosive development. For further information see:
http://www.gresham.ac.uk/lectures-and-events/lessons-we-can-learn-from-the-success-of-the-japanese-growth-system
 and
http://www.gresham.ac.uk/lectures-and-events/the-curious-case-of-the-economist-the-west-forgot-the-life-and-times-of-dr-osamu
(republished at 4.9 above) and
https://medium.com/@georgetaitedwards/the-rough-guide-to-shimomuran-economics-e9dca42c6808
The malign prescriptions of neoclassical economics and its continual depression-producing results cannot continue forever. Shimomuran-Wernerian macroeconomics is the best available path to prosperity once the politicians of the West understand the effectiveness of that option.

Preferably soon."

Comment: The basic difference between what the post-war Japanese Government did and what other more intellectually limited governments did during the post war period was that the Japanese Government enabled the Bank of Japan to create vast flows of credit targeted at [and earmarked for] the restoration and future prosperity of all Japanese businesses.

Japanese SMEs applying for loans to rebuild their businesses found that local banks (to which the BoJ created credit had been "convoyed") were very willing to lend all the money required not only to provide the required capital but also the funds required for the working capital and increased liquidity. That is why Japan recovered so quickly, and one of the major issues Western economists do not generally understand.

760,000 SME premises had been destroyed and 40% of the urban area in the 66 bombed [major] cities in Japan had also been destroyed. Much of Japan's SME activity, then and now, was conducted in the small farm and family homes in the urban areas. Many Japanese businessmen approached the local banks with only one asset - their intelligence and skills - and asked for loans to re-establish their businesses on a "recovery project" basis with no physical collateral except for their devastated assets often on bombed-out land. Japanese local banks not only loaned the money to fund the clear up and replace the destroyed capital assets but also enough money to fund all the required work in progress and finished goods as well providing these SMEs with vast financial resources in the form of very high liquidity.

It is high liquidity in SMEs and in other businesses which creates the business confidence which produces continual high rates of growth and development. Japanese SMEs did not simply replace their small factories and houses (in which much SME production is located) with assets of pre-war quality, they built better and equipped themselves with up-to-date machinery and improved materials to provide an improved productivity and higher growth of future output in the context of a rich high liquidity company - all of it based upon long-term low-interest-rate affordable debt.

The Japanese families which owned SMEs were prosperous as soon as they visited their banks. The vast flows of SME-earmarked credit creation was *the* major factor in the post war recovery of Japan.

The Allies and the Anglosphere had no idea what was happening in post-war Japan and nearly all Anglosphere economists, even now seventy years later, still have no idea. Nearly all capital investment project appraisal in the West is wrong, because it is an analysis of the "returns on investment." All project appraisal in manufacturing industries of whatever scale should take into account the need for funds to provide or maintain high liquidity (or the business might not have the confidence to proceed with the project in the first place) and as well as the need for funding for the capital equipment plus the need to finance the work in progress and the higher levels of finished goods produced by a faster workflow.

Shimomuran-Wernerian economics produces the goods. Neoclassical economics doesn't. The Tokyo Consensus economies are going to dominate the world's future. The Washington Consensus economies are obvious losers in the Darwinian competition for the successful economic adaptions to the challenges of change.
May the inevitable power transition happen peacefully, as it has failed to do historically.

It is of course possible for Western politicians, economists and business leaders to learn, but after more than four decades of trying to bring that change about in Britain, I know such a change won't happen easily. Intelligent politicians are key in that process and politicians of the calibre of FDR, Hiyato Ikeda, John F Kennedy and and Deng Xiao-P'ing are much higher than the usual quality of political leaders. Yet the future of the world depends up such capable leaders. I hope some such will emerge.

4.11 How to restore a fully representative democracy in the United Kingdom

There are four aspects to the full restoration of a fully representative democracy in the United Kingdom. First, there should be the politicisation of the English and Welsh population (as has already occurred in Scotland) and the complete-as-possible reversal of the removal of eligible voters from the parliamentary electoral rolls. Second, there should be an active involvement in that process by all who have an interest in a fully functioning British democratic process. Third, there should be monitoring of results and reports by neutral and objective organisations about the progress of the updating of the electoral registers to inform the public about what is happening. Fourth, an incoming Government based on the full democratic will of the British People should create a British Constitution to ensure that gerrymandering becomes at least as illegal in the United Kingdom as it is in the United States, and should consider other measures to restore widespread prosperity in the United Kingdom. Each of these issues is discussed in turn below. The Chartists in 1842 had one excellent suggestion about how governments could be managed to serve the people better. These issues obviously have a very long history.

4.10.1 the politicisation of the English and Welsh population and the complete-as-possible reversal of the removal of eligible voters from the parliamentary electoral rolls.

The means to reverse the removal of eligible voters from the electoral rolls are already there on the internet. All of the members of the groups who have been disenfranchised by the 2013 IER Act can log on to the internet at www.gov.uk/register-to-vote and they can re-register their basic democratic right to vote. This has to be done by each individual. As the Electoral Commission helpfully comments on their website

"Query about the electoral register or registering to vote?
The Electoral Commission does not compile or maintain the electoral registers.
If you would like to register to vote, find out if you are registered, or change your address on the electoral register you need to contact the Electoral Registration Officer at your local council.
To get their contact details please telephone 020 7271 0500 or visit

our About My Vote website".
The About My Vote website is located at http://
www.aboutmyvote.co.uk/home. That website enables each individual
to find out the appropriate local electoral registration office, which
can then be contacted through the internet or by telephone to register
a vote.

Each elector who contacts their local electoral registration office has
to provide whether by internet or by phone the following details:
1 Full name
2 Address
3 Date of Birth
4 Nationality
5 National Insurance Number
6 Contact details
7 Whether he or she wishes to be on the Open Register (which is a
subset of the Electoral Register which is sold by Government to any
person, company or organisation).

If all the voters were restored to the Parliamentary Electoral Rolls,
the gerrymandering of the Constituency boundaries would become
much more difficult.

4.10.2 Active involvement by all these organisation and groups who are interested in the proper restoration of a fully representative British democracy

Britain at present has the extreme right-wing Government led by
David Cameron but it also enjoys a fully functioning, high quality
and and usually politically neutral bureaucracy. The Electoral
Commission, many high quality Local Authorities, many Quangos
and long-standing charities provide reports, observations and
statistics which are part of the normal information required for the
proper operation of a representative democracy.
The Electoral Commission is Britain's independent elections
watchdog and regulator of party and election finance. The reports it
produces are an objective and invaluable guide to what is actually
going on in the electoral process. Unfortunately nearly all its
recommendations have, during recent years, been entirely ignored by
the Cameron-led Governments.

4.10.3 Monitoring of results and reports by neutral and objective organisations about the progress of the updating of the electoral registers to inform the public about what is happening

If everyone who has been disenfranchised by the 2013 IER act re-instated their electoral rights by contacting their local electoral registration offices through the internet or by phone then the information required to restore the electoral registers to their previous level of accuracy could be achieved within less than 24 hours. I think it would be a glorious democratic revolution if everyone did that because the voter apathy assumptions of this Conservative Government - that the electorate are careless about their right to vote, that the students who have been disenfranchised by the speed of implementation of the 2013 IER legislation are not politically interested enough to re-register, that all those who haven't carefully watched what the Government are doing, all deserve to lose the right to vote - are all wrong.

4.10.4 An incoming non-Conservative Government should create a British Constitution to ensure that gerrymandering becomes at least as illegal in the United Kingdom as it is in the United States.

It is the lack of a constitution which has enabled the gerrymandering of elections since about 1989. The Poll Tax would have been illegal under article 24 of the US constitution. The Cameron Governments have been involved in the greatest denial of democracy so far brought about in their chosen options for implementation of the 2013 IER Act.

The Chartists of 1842 knew some of the things required to ensure a government reflects the will of the people. Their sixth suggestion (see https://en.wikipedia.org/wiki/Chartism) was for "Annual Parliament Elections, because

"Annual Parliament Elections, thus presenting the most effectual check to bribery and intimidation, since as the constituency might be bought once in seven years (even with the ballot), no purse could buy a constituency (under a system of universal suffrage) in each ensuing twelvemonth; and since members, when elected for a year only, would not be able to defy and betray their constituents as now."

The drafting of a British Constitution should consider the principle that a quarter of MPs should be re-elected each year because that change would mean "these members, when elected for a year only, would not be able to defy and betray their constituents as now." That would stop British elections continuing as now - as a year of trickery followed by five years of the betrayal by MPs of the interests of their constituents.

4.10.5 Cameron needs to be continually reminded about what he is and what he has done. The cry of "Cameron the Gerrymanderer" should be heard in the land wherever Cameron shows his face - in parliament, by crowds in Parliament square, and in every public meeting he tries to address. It is essential that protests again his rule should be peaceful and democratically conducted and after he is reminded of what he is and his place in history he should be allowed to speak.
What he is and what he has done will never be forgotten. He belongs in the political hell in which he has placed himself by his actions.

5 Conclusions

5.1 The future of David Cameron

David Cameron is a political, economic and social disaster for the United Kingdom.

He is a political disaster because by his chosen method of implementing the 2013 IER Act he has reversed much of the move towards universal suffrage during the last century, and millions of the the hard-won votes for women, for the young, for immigrants, for the poor and underprivileged living in council housing, have been deliberately removed from the parliamentary electoral roll. His Government is legal but does not have an adequate political mandate to proceed with the reforms which he is progressing. The opinion polls are are better guide to the government Britain should have than the 2015 General Election.

The introduction of Individual Voter Registration (IER) could have been a good thing. As the House of Commons Briefing Paper 6764 , authored by Isobel White and dated 21 July 2015 comments on Page 4

"The Electoral Commission first called for a change to individual electoral registration (IER) in 2003.1 The Commission initially saw the change as being an essential 'building block' for e-enabled elections but individual registration was later seen as an important measure to guard against electoral fraud. The Commission published a report in June 2003, Voting for change: an electoral law modernisation programme, which brought together recommendations from a series of policy papers, including those on registration issues. The Labour Government responded to the report in 2004 and said it was sympathetic to the principles of individual registration but it did not implement the Commission's recommendations, mainly because of concerns about the effect on levels of registration if a system of individual registration was introduced. When individual registration was introduced in Northern Ireland by the Electoral Fraud (Northern Ireland) Act 2002, the numbers on the register there fell by 10.5% although the legislation was seen as successful in reducing electoral fraud."

The major difference between the Labour Government in 2004 and the Cameron-led 2010 Coalition Government and the 2015 Conservative Government is that the former was concerned about the fall in voter registration while the Cameron-led Governments knew that lower voter registration would redound to their partisan benefits. There is no evidence whatsoever that the IER system reduces electoral fraud - that is the only alleged but unproven benefit of an almost entirely politically enforced retrograde system. The problem with the 2013 IER Act is not in its high principles but in its defective gerrymandering implementation. At every stage the Coalition and Conservative Governments have acted to ensure that the Parliamentary Electoral Rolls (PER) once damaged are not fully restored to their previous completeness, and are denied the necessary time to do that. All the recommended measures for the improvement of voter registration in the PER from whatever source have been minimised or ignored for the sake of achieving partisan advantage. There has been and still is a rush to judgement which is profoundly undemocratic and utterly partisan. As the Summary of the above-quoted Commons Briefing Paper 6764 notes
"The Coalition Government announced in 2010 that it was going to speed up the introduction of the new system and the Electoral Registration and Administration Act 2013 made provision for the introduction of IER by 2015."
and "The Electoral Registration and Administration Act 2013 made provision for the transitional period for the introduction of IER to come to an end in 2016. The Act also gave the Secretary of State the power to bring forward the end of the transition to December 2015. The Electoral Commission published a report in June 2015 about the progress of the transition to the new system of IER and did not recommend an early end to the transition period."
But

'On 16 July 2015 the Government laid the Electoral Registration and Administration Act 2013 (Transitional Provisions) Order 2015 before Parliament. This Order will end the transition to IER twelve months early in December 2015; the Government argued that by retaining "carry forward" electors (those who had not yet registered individually under the new system) beyond December 2015, there would be an "unacceptable risk to the accuracy of the register". '

There was a great risk to the Conservative Government if its blitzkrieg implementation of the 2013 IER Act was allowed an extra year to bed in - the PER would be likely to become more complete, with disenfranchised voters re-registering their votes. That would indeed be a risk to the continuation of the Conservative Government. No other risk is identifiable.

The 13% fall in voter registration in the Confirmation Live Run in England and Wales was so great that the Conservatives were likely to be caught, as it were, with their hands in the ballot boxes. A Conservative landslide could be arranged in a general election perhaps in 2020 but it would look very suspicious in May 2015. So

"On 9 January 2015 the Government announced that there would be additional funding of up to £9.8 million in 2015 "to support the costs of activities aimed at increasing the completeness and accuracy of the electoral register"; a further £3 million of additional funding is also being made available for all Electoral Registration Officers in Great Britain to target non IER registered carry forward electors."

But these monies were not earmarked for their stated purposes (despite the 2011 recommendation of the cross-party Political and Constitutional Reform Committee that it should be) and many cash-strapped local authorities were able to use all or part of that trickle of funds to maintain key local services. Trying to locate and register millions of voters who had not been matched with one government database - the DWP one - was a task too large and would take much longer than the four months before the May 2015 General Election. Many of these missing voters were identified and re-registered but many were not, as the results of the General Election when compared with the opinion polls demonstrated. Guarantees were given that all the voters on the December 2013 register would be allowed to vote in the May 2015 General Election, but that did not happen. The new incomplete IER registers were used to enable the election of a Conservative Government.

Other countries, particularly Australia, have managed to introduce IER without disenfranchising a significant percentage of their electorate, as Section 3.5 illustrates.

The Coalition and Conservative implementation of the IER Act 2013 disenfranchises the voters which would, in a fully democratic society, check the damage which David Cameron's Conservative Government could do because his Government would be subsequently voted out. Cameron knows that he cannot be voted out because he is able, through the Government takeover of the Parliamentary Electoral Roll and the removal of millions of voters who do not vote Conservative, to ensure he remains in office despite the will of the people. That's why Cameron ignored the usual democratic discussion of issues in the run-up to the 2015 election - he knew that these issues were not going to decide the election outcome, for he had already fixed the election in his favour through the giant gerrymander of the 2013 IER Act.

The political and social consequences of what he has done, and is doing, do not appear to have occurred to him. The rise of "Blue Labour" through the adoption by the Labour Party of a semi-caring Thatcherism by the Blair and Brown Governments combined with the election of the Coalition Government in 2010 meant that the electorate had no real policy choice between the main British political parties. This was not because the electorate did not want an end to austerity, it was because no such choice was offered to them. The choice in England was between Blair's "Thatcherism light" and the Conservative more right wing Thatcherism. Where a choice was offered, as it was in Scotland by the politically brilliant and deft politician Alex Salmond leading the Scottish National Party, the electorate came to life, voter registration rates soared, voters turned out to vote as never before, and the SNP took every seat in Scotland bar three.

Once the British people understand how thoroughly they have been cheated it seems likely that the English electorate will become as radicalised as the Scots already have been. Throughout history the Conservatives have always voted against the extension of suffrage, voting against universal suffrage, against votes for women, and against votes for the young. An almost entirely establishment press, which is now over 80% foreign-owned, has historically supported these Conservative viewpoints. If history is any guide there will be popular mass movements which may not initially have parliamentary representatives.

To some extent this sea change is already underway in England. The 600,000 membership of the Labor Party, the popular rise of Jeremy Corbyn and his likely election in the current fight for the leadership of the Labour Party is a sign of the rise of a genuinely popular Labour Party.

The previous popular support for the Labour Party has been destroyed by the Blair and Brown Governments which were, in many respects, only Labour in name. Blair has belatedly declared that his programme was the continuation of the "Thatcher Project" and a thoughtful review of that claim is made by Robert Philpott at http://www.huffingtonpost.co.uk/robert-philpot/blair-thatcher-whats-the-difference_b_3083654.html. But however Blair may be re-assessed, he had made an agreement with the City of London - the result of a "cocktail offensive" with the formidable Mo Mowlam - which guaranteed the City's money men that an incoming Labour Government would not legislate against their interests and would be helpful to their reasonable requests. That "cocktail offensive" paved the way for British involvement in the financial meltdown of 2008 because any effective monitoring of the risks taken by British financial institutions had been completely abandoned by Gordon Brown's administration. Labour became "Blue Labour" under Blair, a people's party which lost all its original roots by adopting much of the Conservative party's restrictive monetary and financial targets.

Countries prosper when local banks provide long term loans to local SMEs. That's how the industrial revolution happened, first in Scotland (where the Bank of Scotland was founded to help fund industry, while the Bank of England was founded to help fund the British Government's military overspending). As Wikipedia comments at https://en.wikipedia.org/wiki/Bank_of_Scotland "Where the Bank of England was established specifically to finance defence spending by the English government, the Bank of Scotland was established by the Scottish government to support Scottish business, and was prohibited from lending to the government without parliamentary approval."

In Scotland and England and South Wales there were local banks which funded industrial development from about 1750 until the mid-1880s depression which produced the bank amalgamation movements. The destruction of British industrial supremacy occurred because the bank amalgamation movement destroyed the 800 or so local so-called "Country Banks" operating in the year 1800 with the result that savings flowed into the big six banks in the capital. These big six banks drain the lifeblood of the future - over 80% of the mobilisable savings of the people - into London and although they act as drains for saving they do not act, as Professor Glynn Davies told the Wilson Committee, as taps for industrial investment. So Britain declines and the British politicians have seen their major function as the management of that decline, not knowing any better.

David Cameron is an economic disaster because he and his government have no idea about how to bring about economic growth, nor do any of his advisors. His government are pursuing policies which have no chance whatsoever of increasing the wealth or welfare of the people of the United Kingdom. Like Thatcher, he is trying to "attempt vast transformations with minority support." Less than 37% of the voters and less than a quarter of the total electorate voted for the Cameron Government, which has no popular grass roots support for what it is doing.

David Cameron is a social disaster because his policies are aimed at destroying the pre-existing social contract between the Government of Britain and its people. Despite his pre-election promise that the NHS would be "safe in his hands" his minister, David Hunt, has privatised a large section of the NHS without the usual parliamentary consideration of the effects of that decision. Millions of people are suddenly being denied their benefits without any warning and without the possibility of a genuine review. The contempt and derision being ladled out by the DWP to any protesters to their cuts in benefits are quite unprecedented by any Government Department. Cameron is operating a kind of blitzkrieg Government, rapidly implementing socially destructive, poverty-increasing policies without any of the usual due regard for the duty of care towards the British people. This has added a new note of Government administrative incompetence and utter callousness to appallingly bad policy. The frequent and successful legal challenges to the dismantling of the welfare net illustrate this. The Independent Newspaper has just listed the ten worst decisions the Cameron Government have taken so far, during their first 100 days. See http://www.independent.5co.uk/news/uk/politics/david-camerons-first-100-days-10-of-the-worst-measures-introduced-by-the-government-so-far-10457028.html.

David Cameron often does not seem to understand the implications of his own policies. If the British Parliament is not always a unitary body, with equal powers for all MPs, and can sometimes make English MPs the only ones who can vote on English matters, then two or three separate   bodies need to be set up. EVEL - English MPs Voting for English Laws - should be matched by SVSL (Scottish Votes for Scottish Laws) with NIVNIL for Northern Ireland and WVWL for Wales.

Both the Conservatives and Labour Parties in parliament are currently deluding themselves. Cameron's Conservatives are imagining that, with the help of 15 very rich men (14 of whom live in London) who provide 84% of the party's income and with a compliant media, they can stay in power indefinitely in the damaged democracy resulting from the 2013 IER Act.

The Official Labour Party seems to be acting as if the outcome of the next election will be decided by the policies it adopts and not by the reduced 2013 IER-produced selectorate and is tearing itself apart on the issue of whether to continue following a Blairite "Blue Labour" agenda or an end-to-austerity programme under Jeremy Corbyn.

The scale of the Cameron's gerrymandering in the United Kingdom has three major implications.

First, the sheer extent of the gerrymandering - 5.5 million voters initially in the Confirmation Live Run (CLR) plus up to 7 million voters after December 2015 plus the reduction in new just-18 year old voters (the "attainers") suggests that about 12.8 million people who would have had a right to vote under the previous HER system have had their voting rights questioned and often denied.

The Troubles in Northern Ireland are widely believed to have begun because of the gerrymandering in the Northern Irish local authorities in about 2003. Cameron's gerrymandering through the 2013 IER Act is on a greater scale than that which occurred in Northern Ireland and could produce similar levels of discontent, *this time in England.*

The major point in a democracy is that the elected parliament is meant to represent and reflect the will of the people. The 2013 IER Act, by acting as a selection device, mainly selecting Conservative voters, sets up a Government which does not represent or reflect the will of the people, because so many of the people have been disenfranchised. That Act therefore paves the way for a permanent state of public disobedience.

Cameron may have made Britain unmanageable in the same way the Northern Irish administration created the Troubles. The public discontent on the streets of Britain may continue without the possibility of any democratic change of government through the ballot box, which has been effectively disabled by the Cameron Government. Judging by the opinion polls, the protests on the street have more democratic legitimacy than the Cameron Government. These protests are not the cry of the losers at the ballot box but the legitimate voices of an electorate which knows that it has somehow been tricked.

Second, the Cameron Government programme has no democratic validity in the sense that that the Government has a flawed mandate and does not represent the democratic will of the people. It is a living constitutional crisis. All of its actions are not based on a valid democratic mandate because the proper operation of the democratic system has been disabled.

But there is no law against gerrymandering in the United Kingdom. The Cameron Government is legal but has an absolutely flawed mandate with no right whatsoever to act against the interests of the people it has disenfranchised, but that seems to be what this Government's actions are about.

The Conservatives may well believe they are the only legitimate party of government in Britain and that they are morally superior to their opponents because they are the party of privilege. Cameron has even described himself (purely for the purpose of electioneering) as belonging to the caring compassionate section of the Conservative party. His behaviour however completely invalidates his self-description. Cameron is the most divisive leader, fronting the most divisive right wing Government, that the UK has ever known.

David Cameron tried to detoxify the Conservative Party before the 7 May election by claiming that the "NHS would be safe in his hands" and that he was in the old tradition of compassionate, caring Conservatism. His actions have belied these claims. The destruction of   welfare state, once again piloted in Scotland, has produced very odd and callous DWP behaviour - the "Suicide guidance" given to benefits staff to cope with desperate calls from people being denied survival funds being just one example. See http://www.heraldscot-land.com/news/homenews/13620988._Suicide_guidance__given_-to_benefits_staff_preparing_for_desperate_calls_on_welfare_reform/?ref=rss

There was one Parliamentary Committee which could have and should have prevented the rise of David Cameron's gerrymandering. That was the Political and Constitutional Reform Committee (PRC), which was abolished by the Conservative party whips on 26 May 2015. That Committee had a mandate for the examination of the way the British democracy operated. It should have acted as a brake and a commentator upon the implementation of the 2013 IER and on the loss of registered voters and their effect on on the 2015 General Election. It was intending to do that. Graham Allen, MP, was the chair of that Committee, told Andrew Blick about his intended programme if he (Graham) was re-elected to chair that Committee.

And Andrew Blick reported at the Democratic Audit UK Website (http://www.democraticaudit.com/?p=13360) in an article entitled

The abolition of the Political and Constitutional Reform Committee is a loss to Parliament and British democracy about Graham Allen's programme:

"To get an idea of what we will be missing, here is the work programme that Graham [Allen] has told me he would have liked to have pursued, had the whips not abolished PCRC, and had he been elected by the whole House as its Chair;

1. Parliamentary Boundaries.
2. English votes for English laws.
3. The democratic implications of Devolution in England.
4. The Human Rights Act.
5. Review of 2015 General Election with respect to Voter Engagement and Registration.
6. Constitutional Implications of Scottish legislation emerging from the Smith Commission.
7. A Constitutional Convention for the UK.
8. 800th anniversary of Magna Carta and the future of a Written/Unwritten Constitution.

We should all regret this loss to Parliament and to democracy."

All of these items are issues which neither David Cameron nor the Conservative Party would like to be investigated. All of these items are interesting, but the first, fifth, seventh and eighth would have highlighted the denial of democracy inherent in the Conservative Government's behaviour.

Very relevant also are the views of four experts (Louise Thompson, Lecturer in Politics, University of Surrey; Graham Allen, MP, Chair of the PRC 2010-15; Richard Berry, Research Associate, Democratic Audit UK; and Andrew Blick, Lecturer in Politics and Contemporary History, Kings College London) on the effects of abolishing the PRC at http://www.democraticaudit.com/?p=13418. As Louise Thompson reports:

"Although some select committee reports do see a tardy response from the government, the frequency with which this occurred towards the PCRC suggests that its members may have been doing too good a job at putting government plans under the microscope. With so much more constitutional reform now on the agenda, there is a considerable gap in Parliament's scrutiny mechanisms. If it is not the PCRC holding the government to account, it will now be up to individual MPs to try to adequately scrutinise these plans. Doing so without the resources of a select committee will be very difficult indeed."

As Graham Allen comments

"The need for Parliamentary accountability and public scrutiny on democratic change is more necessary after the election not less. The Union faces a crisis internally and in its relations with Europe, Devolution in England is now a pressing political issue, Parliament needs to find its role, the Human Rights Act faces abolition, disenchantment with politics and democracy and the public questioning of the legitimacy of Government is at an all-time high. Parliament needs to play its full part in addressing these problems and not be denied effective means to do so by Government."

Richard Berry, Research Associate of Democratic Audit UK says that

"The abolition of the Political and Constitutional Reform Committee represents a significant loss to UK democracy," and Andrew Blick comments on what the PRC did:

"It carried out groundbreaking investigations into previously neglected areas, including a consideration of the possibility of a code for independent local government. Its inquiry into the idea of a written constitution for the United Kingdom was the first ever to be conducted."

It is very clear that the objective of the Cameron-led Conservative Government is to implement further gerrymandering and constitutional change in Britain without the scrutiny of the PRC.

Government actions often have unforeseen side effects. In my opinion both Cameron and the Conservative Party have been re-toxified beyond all possibility of recovery by their partisan implementation of the 2013 IER Act and by their stated intention to gerrymander the constituency boundaries on the basis of a politically reduced electorate so as to deny the Labour Party, however led, from forming a government for decades.

5.2 Where there is no vision, the people perish (proverbs 29:18)

At location 4442 of 6953 of the Kindle version of his book "Britain Since 1900 - A Success Story?" Lord Robert Skidelsky comments:

"The Thatcher governments from 1979 to 1990 demolished the ruined post-war settlement. Of its three pillars - the full-employment commitment, the mixed economy and the welfare state - only the third remained standing."

David Cameron has set himself to destroy the third pillar of the post-war settlement - the welfare state which Thatcher left standing. He has no mandate whatsoever to do that but because he has a parliamentary majority he believes that's enough. It isn't.

Neither he nor his party have any positive vision of the future of the British people. And that Conservative majority is due to the largest gerrymandering ever practised in the UK, so not only does he have no positive vision of the future of the people of Britain, his government lacks democratic legitimacy.

The British Government has a duty of care to provide adequate food and shelter for its population. If the economy does not provide the essential employment for the people in all regions of the UK then the welfare net has, during the post-war period, provided the essential safeguarding of the disadvantaged people in order to ensure their survival.

The Independent newspaper has reported upon David Cameron's first 100 days and the worst ten measures so far introduced (see http://www.independent.co.uk/news/uk/politics/david-camerons-first-100-days-10-of-the-worst-measures-introduced-by-the-government-so-far-10457028.html). These worst ten measures are
1 The Child Poverty target - that is, the legally-binding target to eliminate Child Poverty by 2020 - has ben scrapped.
2 There has been a cut in working tax credits so that families with more than two children will not receive tax credits or housing benefits for third or more children, reducing benefits for any child over two by £2,780 a year.

3 The "Green Deal" which was meant to enable householders to instal energy-saving measures has been scrapped

4 There has been a cut in benefit for asylum seekers which Charities have warned would result in asylum seekers being unable to afford food and clothes for their families.

5 Maintenance grants for students from low income families have been replaced by higher student loans.

6 Universities will be allowed to raise fees above £9,000 a year at the rate of inflation from 2017/18 if they show good quality.

7 Strict laws banning public sector strikes unless there is a vote of more than 40% for key workers and 50% for non-key workers.

8 Halting railway improvements by pausing key parts of the £38.5bn Network Rail upgrade programme.

9 Reviewing the Freedom of Information Act under Jack Straw, who thinks it needs reviewed

10 Further lowering the benefit cap for large families - down by £6,000 a year (to £20,000 from £26,000) for non-London families and down to £23,000 in the capital.

Cameron's vision of the future of Britain is a country where, due to Government vindictiveness against their non-supporters, millions of children are starving, millions of people denied benefits cannot afford food and shelter, and millions of ill people cannot afford medical attention due to the destruction of the NHS and its rebirth as a privatised medical priority service for the rich. The denial of monies required for survival will produce a desperation which will cause a major and quasi-permanent crime wave. The informal economy will increase to provide people with illegal jobs in the drugs, prostitution and protection industries, and these may become the major source of job creation in much of the country. Protest movements and ongoing civil unrest will become a permanent feature of British society as these movements provide individuals with the essential satisfaction of involvement in a social group. Britain now has some favelas, tent housing in its major cities to accommodate some of the people who no longer receive benefits. These might spread everywhere despite legal action against them. There is no need for that to happen. Cameron's malign destruction of the welfare state and the NHS is underway but could be stopped in its tracks as sections 4.3 to 4.10 illustrate.

All British Members of Parliament and of the House of Lords should hang their heads in shame at these appalling results. The Mother of Parliaments has been prostituted for partisan ends. All the checks and balances allegedly part of the British system of Government seem to have been asleep at their posts to allow this monstrosity of misrepresentation to happen. The Political and Constitutional Reform Committee (PRC) was abolished by the Conservative party whips on 26 May 2015, so no deep scrutiny of constitutional changes is now possible by Parliament.

In my considered opinion all of the gerrymandering done by David Cameron and the Conservative Party is likely to backfire. David Cameron by gerrymandering the Parliamentary Electoral Rolls and by planning to gerrymander the constituency boundaries has gone far too far in undermining the democratic foundations of British society.

David Cameron is leading an unjust, unpopular and undemocratic government. His Government has no valid democratic mandate for the appalling policies it is implementing. The Conservative Government is inept because there is none of the usual parliamentary consideration and the duty of care in the implementation of Government policy. That lack of consideration and callousness seems to be a reflection of David Cameron's personality.

I believe David Cameron has made his leadership and his party a toxic brand. The British people would never vote for any Government which used and planned to use its power to permanently disable the normal operations of British democracy.

It may take some time for the British people to restore these normal operations but everything that David Cameron has done, goes against the trend of the greater democratic mandate and the increasing democracy in Britain during the last 172 years. I am sure that a fully functioning British democracy will eventually be re-established regardless of what Mr Cameron and the Conservative Party have done or plan to do.

The only question is when.

Appendix 1: 14th April 2015 article outlining "How to Create an Economic Miracle in the UK or Elsewhere" previously published at https://medium.com/@georgetaitedwards/how-to-create-an-economic-miracle-d2ffa95e6c73

The following republished article lists the ten key actions which could make the United Kingdom (or any other nation which developed an intelligent government and competent economists) a high-growth economy.

There are many people, some of whom are economists, and many well-meaning groups on the internet who have grasped the reality that fiat money costs nothing to produce. These individuals and groups often do not understand the natural complexity in the use of credit creation, about how best to use credit creation to facilitate higher economic growth through credit creation; about how important it is to loan funds very cheaply (in both interest and long-term low cost repayments which are affordable to the lender); to provide enough SME and industrial funding to create the liquidity levels which lie at the root of business confidence; to manage inflation by setting the interest rate equal to the rise in price of factory-gate goods; and various other matters. The purpose of the following essay is to summarise all the ten key activities required to create and manage a high growth, low inflation economy in the UK. Some parts of the following article might seem out of date, but the specific suggestions are illustrative rather than still available. For example the TSB has now been sold to a Spanish bank. The fact remains that any growth policy in the UK or anywhere else would require a distribution system to a knowledgable local bank network to get the centrally-created clearing bank funds to local SMEs, as the German Sparkassen system does. And each economy should support their cultural uniqueness and local talent, as the BBC at its best does.

"1 Introduction This is a more extensive "bare bones" summary about how to make the United Kingdom a high growth economy by briefly listing the major

Government legislation which is required to bring about that result. This version provides references that the "Ten Commandments" Version doesn't.

2 Purpose The primary purpose of this essay is to present the 2015 incoming UK Government with an effective programme for reversing British economic decline. But although this essay is focused on the British situation, the activities listed below shifted into a locally relevant form are a political programme for rapid economic development by any intelligent government, and a secondary purpose of this essay is to provide that. A third purpose is to provide the required economic technology to deal with national disasters through no-cost investment credit creation national programmes. Finally this programme is founded upon Shimomuran-Wernerian macroeconomics and requires that mental upgrading in understanding to see how these activities all fit together in a "real-world" fresh machinery of effective Government. [See the Long Finance Spring Conference lectures at Gresham College http://www.gresham.ac.uk/lectures-and-events/the-curious-case-of-the-economist-the-west-forgot-the-life-and-times-of-dr-osamu and http://www.gresham.ac.uk/lectures-and-events/lessons-we-can-learn-from-the-success-of-the-japanese-growth-system]

3 Activities to Ensure High UK Economic Growth Market forces and neoclassical economics do not promote adequate rates of economic development. The five major British Clearing Banks collect some 90% of deposits [see Slide 28 of Richard Werner's 3 March 2015 Long Finance Gresham College presentation at http://www.gresham.ac.uk/sites/default/files/richard_werner_-_gresham_-college_3_mar_2015.pdf] and drain local savings to London for whatever purpose is currently fashionable, but they do not provide local taps for funding SME or company investment. This is entirely different from the supportive way the hundreds of British banks behaved at the time of the industrial revolution. [For much more detail on this issue see my summary of Professor Glynn Davies' 1977 First Submission in evidence to the Wilson Committee, 1977 at pages 30–38 of my book "The Role of Banks in Economic Development—The Economics of Industrial Resurgence" (Foreword by Harold Lever) The Macmillan Press Ltd, London, 1987. Also relevant to these issues is the book John C Carrington and George T Edwards, "Reversing Economic Decline" The Macmillan Press Ltd, 1981] The British financial system needs to be changed to support local invention and factory innovation and decentralised economic development as it once did, and to enable the continuation of a more developed   economy of abundant capital and much higher economic growth rates. That can be done through the following ten main Government actions.

3.1 Nationalise the Bank of England (BoE) and Legislate for it to Promote British Economic Development All of the economic miracle economies—Manchuria during the 1920s-30s, FDR's USA 1938–44, Japan 1945–74, South Korea 1950–73, Taiwan 1950–73 and China 1975-present day—have been and (with the exception of the USA) still are Investment Credit Creation (ICC) economies, and during their high growth period have created no-cost investment credit at the Central Bank (CB) mainly by re-discounting SME and some business bank loans to create the funds required for further waves of SME and business investment. [See http://en.wikipedia.org/wiki/German_public_bank and https://medium.com/@georgetaitedwards/dr-osamu-shimomura-1910-89-his-major-achievements-be2ad3e39e77] No-cost investment credit creation is the fundamental policy which enables high economic growth. That policy is not possible (as Dr Osamu Shimomura and Professor Richard Werner have both independently argued) without the subsidiary of a compliant CB which can play a positive part in promoting national economic development. [For the arguments of Dr Osamu Shimomura, see page 24 of The Political Economy of Japanese Monetary Policy, Thomas Cargill and others, The MIT Press, Cambridge, Massachusetts and London, which is also available to review on the internet at http://books.google.co.uk/books id=f3s47HWB8g8C&printsec=frontcover&source=gbs_ge_summary_r&cad=0#v=onepage&q&f=false and for these of Richard Werner see p337 of his second book"new paradigm in macroeconomics" Palgrave Macmillan, 2005]

3.2 Nationalise the Trustee Savings Bank (TSB) or create a distributive bank system providing long-term loans for SMEs All successful miracle economies have not only had a compliant CB but also an effective domestic funds distribution system to convoy the centrally-created CB credit down to local SME level. The TSB could provide that, and can be re-organised into becoming hundreds of quasi-independent local banks with Sparkasssen objectives (for the support of local prosperity and funding of local SMEs).
[See http://en.wikipedia.org/wiki/German_public_bank] The UK Clearing Banks, throughout the last 130 years, have increasingly drained local savings for central purposes and have become totally resistant to change and not at all interested in helping UK industry prosper, and have frequently argued against any such involvement.

[See Chapter 5 (pages 118–173) of George T Edwards, The Role of Banks in Economic Development, Foreword by Harold Lever, The Macmillan Press (now The Palgrave Press) London, 1987 for Clearing Bank behaviour during 1975–85, and Peter Scott and Dr Lucy Newton's paper *"Jealous monopolists? British banks and responses to the Macmillan Gap during the 1930s"* at https://www.reading.ac.uk/web/FILES/management/036.pdf]

3.3 Provide Low-Repayment-Cost Investment Credit for Local SMEs via the TSB [or other local banking network}

The key activity which the previous two activities enable is the provision of affordable low-interest rate long-term loans for SMEs. [For a detailed discussion about the repayment costs of capital during the early 1970s, see John C Carrington and George T Edwards, *Financing Industrial Investment*, Macmillan, London 1979.] BoE window guidance (providing the rediscounting of pre-existing SME and manufacturing company loans for only the TSB up to stated monthly limits) can provide the further funds to be convoyed from their point of creation at the BoE window guidance to their use to improve the liquidity, work in progress, finished goods and updated plant and equipment in locally based UK SMEs and manufacturing companies. The cost of funds to the TSB [or loan distributing bank] at the BoE should be set as equal to the annual factory gate inflation rate in the price of goods or 2% whichever is the lower. The TSB should set the cost of ten year to 20-year loans to SMEs and manufacturing companies at 1% above the BoE rate.

3.4 Set Up Regional Development Agencies (RDAs) and Regional Development Banks (RDBs)

Government needs to be fully informed about the nature and extent of SME and company commercial activity in the UK regions, each of which needs a Regional Development Agency and a Regional Development Bank to identify and support the rapid growth of SMEs, manufacturing excellence and some commercial service activities in the regions of the UK. Many major SME inventions grow through factory floor innovation to become much larger than their local TSB branches can support, and as in Germany, regional banks should be of a scale to enable the funding of the major industrial and commercial companies in each region. [See https://medium.com/@georgetaitedwards/shimomuran-economics-is-the-most-significant-advance-ever-made-in-economic-understanding-and-the-e540e58bf270 and see Slide 28 of Richard Werner's 3 March

2015 Long Finance Gresham College presentation at http://www.gresham.ac.uk/sites/default/files/richard_werner_-_gresham_college_3_mar_2015.pdf]

3.5 Set up an Economic Planning Agency (EPA) and a National Development Bank (NDB) in the Office of the Prime Minister

Every government needs to be better informed by a competent advice system which realistically assesses the economic history, the current circumstances, and the future prospects of its key industries. That planning agency can collect local TSB and RDA information and perpetually monitor local, regional and national economic activity, providing a wealth of relevant policy details about the continually changing economic and physical environment, and propose recommendations for action based upon real world data. The major capital programmes of the UK—national flood defences, including the raising of the London Barrage, the restoration and future defence of the Somerset levels, and all other defences against rising tides need to be coordinated and financed centrally, as does the roads system, new town and city developments, airports and high speed rail projects and various aspects of national security.

The current Coalition Government have produced such a stream of propaganda to suit its immediate political purposes that they are living in a dream world with no connection to the real one perhaps an inevitable result of practising the prescriptions of the unreal theoretical world of neoclassical economics.

The people of the United Kingdom have no prospect of a prosperous future through the continuation of a policy of misery-inducing government budget cuts. The closure of major UK companies and/or their sale to foreign buyers should generally become a thing of the past. The Government should have a Disaster Recovery Programme to cope with extreme weather and other disasters as well as a prevention programme to limit the extent of these events. The EPA and NDB can assist in that.

3.6 Ensure Business, TSB, RDA, RIB, EPA, NIB and Government Competence in Understanding Investment Credit and Capital Projects

The Treasury's Green Book, excellent in so many respects, stresses capital expenditure as the only major aspect of a project (see the Green Book, para 5.54 and Box 11) and does not recommend project evaluation should include the costs of financing of the additional liquidity, work in progress, and higher levels of finished goods which are essential operational aspects of any major goods producing capital project. That means that the Green Book is an inadequate document for the proper evaluation of these capital projects. All capital projects carry a degree of risk and non-government projects are only undertaken by firms if the firm has (or can acquire) adequate liquidity to survive that associated risk, and for large projects and most projects that assumption is wrong. Capital projects usually involve an increase in labour productivity and faster product throughput, which requires more financing for material inputs, finished goods and work in progress. All future evaluations of goods-producing "capital" projects should include the financing of much higher liquidity, more work in progress, more finished goods and more staff training to ensure the success of the considered project. Many British firms have modernised their equipment on the basis of an incomplete Green Book type analysis only to go bankrupt through inadequate liquidity, often due to the unforeseen under-provision of input materials and the over-trading route to bankruptcy. Liquidity is paramount over profitability and a notable feature of all economic miracle economies has been higher company borrowing to finance liquidity, with higher investment in input materials, work in progress and finished goods. This is not a theory that reality must be understood at all levels. Previous UK Governments have sometimes funded the major capital requirements of a project (e.g. BMC, DMC) only to have the company and the project founder on liquidity, work in progress and over-trading considerations. There is no point in evaluating the rare of return on a major new capital investment without taking into account the liquidity requirements of the operation of that new facility, but that is what the Green Book does. A minor rewriting which would have major results - is required.

3.7 Legislate for wage and salary increases to be awarded in two tranches with the second tranche paid via a local TSB [or other distributive] Bank Account

Legislation should be introduced to require all future wage and salary increases to be partly (c50%) paid as an increase in weekly or monthly wages or salaries and the rest as an annual 1 November bonus as a bank account credit in the local TSB. [This is a key part of inflation control in Shimomuran economics—see paragraph 3 of https://medium.com/@georgetaitedwards/dr-osamu-shimomura-1910-89-his-major-achievements-be2ad3e39e77] That policy limits the immediate major source of inflation, encourages productivity improvements, and increases personal savings because a high proportion of lump-sum bonuses are usually saved. The increase in personal saving can provide the recipient banks with additional funds for whatever purposes these banks promote. All bonuses should be legislated to be paid to persons via a local Trustee Savings Bank account   because only these banks will have the legislated productive purpose of assisting local SME growth. Employees should have the option of retaining their existing primary bank if they so choose although many will obviously prefer to transfer their accounts to a useful local bank and away from the existing central, useless Central London and Scottish Clearing Banks.

3.8 Restore the Government's Duty of Care Towards All The People

Restore all the £20bn cuts of the Coalition Government and make it as if the Coalition Government had never existed. The cuts in support payments to the unemployed and others are entirely due to a Coalition Government which only understands making economies and knows nothing about wealth creation and positive macroeconomics. These cuts are completely unjustified and are causing great difficulty among the poorer and disadvantaged sections of the population which the Coalition   Government regard as not their supporters. (See the sixth article out of nine by Bryan Gould and George Tait Edwards http://londonprogressivejournal.com/article/view/2128 for more detail on this policy.)

3.9 Properly Fund the Major Aspects of British Culture Britain has rotted from the head during the five years of Coalition dominance. The leaders of the Coalition Government—the Prime Minister David Cameron, the Deputy Prime Minister Nick Clegg, the

Chancellor of the Exchequer George Osborne—have no idea whatsoever about how to create wealth or accelerate economic growth. The United Kingdom since the end of the Second World War until the election of Thatcher in 1979 was a cultural beacon of Western civilisation. It can be all that once again if there are proper funding arrangements for the key institutions of British culture. There are many underfunded aspects of the United Kingdom which Shimomuran-Wernerian macroeconomics can fund more adequately, and four of the major ones are listed in paras 3.9.1 to 3.9.4 below.

3.9.1 Adequately fund the NHS The NHS is one of the fundamental institutions for ensuring good health for the people in the United Kingdom and all the instruments for the legal privatisation of the NHS should be nullified. The NHS should be restored to its true function as a service free at the point of use for all the British people and not a two-tier service offering rationed care within inadequate budgets for the poor and an Americanised private and very expensive health service for the rich. Adequate NHS budgets should be set in the booming Shimomuran-Wernerian economy of the UK.

3.9.2 Restore free higher education in England Since the educational reforms of John Knox, the Scots have contributed to British and world culture well above their numbers. Alex Salmond says that his proudest boast is that he has maintained the centuries-long tradition of free higher education in Scotland. A higher education—free to all who can benefit from it—is the essential foundation of a flourishing civilisation and it should be available in England and Wales and Northern Ireland as well as in Scotland.

3.9.2 Restore funding to the Arts Council During the last four centuries of natural socio-economic evolution, Britain has been culturally significant as a leading nation within the matrix of Western European civilisation. Its voice has been crippled due to the lack of national funding and the inevitable focus of that reduced funding on the London area. British culture is not a South-East England phenomena and support for culture and the arts should be provided regionally. The Arts Council is trying to do its best in supporting the arts in the regions but that might be impossible given the reduced funding. The recent collapse of part of the ceiling of the Apollo Theatre in London on the spectators is but one sign of the rot in adequate funding even for the buildings providing cultural facilities.

3.9.3 Provide adequate levels of independent funding to the BBC

During the last five years the BBC has turned into the mouthpiece of the Coalition government. Its coverage now lacks any objective focus. Any and all protests about Government legislation has been under-reported by the BBC, and many government-supporting persons seem unaware of that. The coverage of the Scottish Referendum and of the SNP has been the broadcasting of Government-supporting misinformation and the suppression of the facts which continues to this day and the natural response of the SNP to the BBC's misbehaviour is to demand an independent Scottish Broadcasting Corporation which could more fairly report upon and perhaps reflect the views of the Scottish Government and not only these of Westminster. National disasters such as local flooding (the Somerset levels, in the Severn Valley and in Northern England) are given initial prominence but not followed up in BBC news which is meant to have a regional focus. The BBC World Service is but a shadow of its former self. BBC news should not follow the lead of the British news media which is largely foreign owned, or operated by non-UK or offshore domiciled individuals and largely reflecting the interests of the rich. The BBC should have a status based upon an independent charter with legally separate funding which permits a more objective news voice. The mainly regionally-based BBC entertainment programmes are still excellent and it is the chartered objectives to inform and to educate which have almost completely failed.

3.9.4 Adequately Fund R&D in Companies and Universities

The British are among the most inventive people in the world but the government-provided R&D funding has diminished considerably and should be restored.

3.10 Use EPA Annual Economic Reviews to Actively Manage the UK's Economic Future

All miracle economies have begun in a realistic evaluation of their existing circumstances and have developed a successful and highly detailed economic plan to put the prerequisites of economic success into place. It was two Japanese electrical engineers—Saburo Okita and Tonosuke Goto—who drafted the highly realistic 1945/6 report "The Basic Problems of Japan's Economic Reconstruction" which led to Japan's rapid post war recovery [see https://medium.com/@georgetaitedwards/how-japan-zoomed-from-war-devastation-into-prosperity-1945-52-92cad27eea81] and the structure of that report is a model for the economic re-appraisals down to the present day. [That report is available in English—see Saburo Okita, editor, Postwar Reconstruction of the Japanese Economy, University of Tokyo Press, 1992.] FDR's 1938–44 economic miracle began by rapidly discovering where the US economy was failing to produce the materials required to win the war and then setting up powerful committees with access to the financial capacity to remedy the identified deficiencies. [See http://londonprogressivejournal.com/article/view/1507/fdrs-american-economic-miracle-or-the-first-economic-bomb-the-usa-from-to-part] After the Bank of Japan's disastrous two decades of trying neoclassical economics (from 1991 to 2010) Shinzo Abe is once again attempting to re-establish Shimomuran economics in Japan, and as usual in an economy practising realistic economics his proposals are for the creation of a "Japan of abundant capital". [See http://www.kantei.go.jp/foreign/96_abe/statement 201304/19speech_e.html for the full text of Abe's 19 April 2013 speech to the Japan National Press Club] If anyone doubts the value of an EPA, even the most cursory comparison of the UK's Social Trends with any copy of the EPA's Economic Survey of Japan would remove such doubts. The information the UK collects is primarily after-the-event economic and social data which is interesting but not particularly useful while the "Economic Survey" is full of useful explanatory tables showing what is happening in Japanese firms and what connections may exist between various economic statistics. The function of "Social Trends" is to provide a commentary on British social (mainly consumer) trends, the function of the EPA's "Economic Survey(s)" is to provide a knowledge of business results arising from Japanese Government economic policies with a view to providing the basis for further action, if required.

4 Discussion The future prosperity of nations is too great an issue to be left to chance. No matter how hopeless the economic position of a country may seem, its people can attain much better standards of living through effective government action to convert local inventions, usually made by individuals in SMEs, into factory-floor innovations. The ingenuity of mankind and womankind seems almost infinite but if arrangements are not put into place to foster and fund that ingenuity the economic game is lost.

4.1 Theoretical and Realistic Economics There are two major traditions in economics, the theoretical and the realistic. The climax of theoretical economics and the mindset within which most Western trained economists are trapped is the castle in the air of neoclassical economics. As Wikipedia puts it "Neoclassical economics is also often seen as relying too heavily on complex mathematical models, such as those used in general equilibrium theory, without enough regard to whether these actually describe the real economy." The simple fact is that they don't. Wikipedia adds "A famous answer to this criticism is Milton Friedman's claim that theories should be judged by their ability to predict events rather than by the realism of their assumptions" [See http://en.wikipedia.org/wiki/Neoclassical_e-conomics]. But neoclassical economics has now been tried for over a third of a century throughout the entire Washington Consensus area and has utterly failed to produce the frequently predicted and promised prosperity, and has instead led to widespread misery. The dominance of the Anglosphere has enabled Washington economic advisors to push their unrealistic views down the throats of non-Western nations and has led to widespread derision about major Washington institutions (eg the IMF, World Bank, OECD etc.). Western politicians often appear quite crazy because they are usually acting in good faith from the best economic advice available to them from their neoclassical "experts". These politicians are pursuing policies which cannot possibly work but which have caused lost decades and an economic doldrums despite their highly developed economies and their inventive, innovative and well-educated people, because neoclassical economics does not adequately relate to the real world.There is an alternative realistic economics, based upon the tradition of "the German Historical School of Economics" [See http://en.wikipedia.org/wiki/Historical_school_of_economics] That alternative focuses on a real-world historical analysis about what works and what is actually happening. As Wikipedia comments "The historical school held that history was the key source of knowledge about human actions and economic matters, since economics was culture-specific, and hence not generalizable over space and time. The school rejected the universal validity of economic theorems. They saw economics as resulting from careful empirical and historical analysis instead of from logic and mathematics. The school also preferred reality, historical, political, and social, as well as economic, to mathematical modelling." Wikipedia adds "In the Anglosphere (English speaking countries), the historical school is perhaps the least known and least understood approach to the study of economics, because it differs radically from the now-dominant Anglo-American analytical point of view. Yet, the historical school forms the basis—both in theory and in practice—of the social market economy for many decades the dominant economic paradigm in most countries of continental Europe. The historical school is also a source of Joseph Schumpeter's dynamic, change-oriented, and innovation-based economics."The major area in the world where the German Historical School of Economics prevails is the "Tokyo-sphere" or the Tokyo Consensus Area where Shimomuran no-cost investment credit economics underlies the creation of economies of "abundant capital" [See https://medium.-com/@georgetaitedwards/the-rough-guide-to-shimomuran-eco-nomics-e9dca42c6808] Professor Richard Werner of Southampton University has extended the Shimomuran analysis by placing it into an overall credit-creation framework [see that framework at slide 23 of http://www.gresham.ac.uk/sites/default/files/richard_werner_-_gresham_college_3_mar_2015.pdf] and the most thorough example of modern realistic economics is Shimomuran-Wernerian macroeconomics.

4.2 A few future developments There is no such thing as the post-industrial economy. The advance of science and the consequent embedded technology in new products produces a continual improvement in the efficiency, effectiveness and usability of all products in all areas of human endeavour. The non-polluting, much safer automatic driver-less cars, buses and trucks of perhaps a generation from now will bear scant resemblance to the first invented and mass-produced cars. Totally automatic takeoff transit and landing aircraft will make hijacking impossible and only baggage all-automatic flights will make no-baggage flights much safer. 3D printing will open up an entire system of personal customising of most products. No-glasses 3D TV and Microsoft's hololens will revolutionise home entertainment and virtual business meetings will become commonplace. The 3D printing of human organs pioneered by Hitachi but being developed in many locations will make donor transplants based upon recipient DNA a major industry of the future, as Shinzo Abe has recognised. Human lifespan, based upon medical discovery, is likely to increase substantially (and the beginnings of that are already obvious in the new death control drugs in widespread use in the West) and there will be much higher national GDPs due to the longer work-span in all developed economies. All of that and much else will need effective, caring and competent governments, the total abandonment of neoclassical economics and the complete retraining of all Western economists about Shimomuran-Wernerian economics which this article partly sets out.

4.3 The Sustainability Shift in Economic Activities The power source for most future economic activities is electrical energy. The generation of electrical energy from renewable sources—wind, hydro-electrical, wave and solar sources—looks adequate to meet nearly all the usual economic needs. Shimomuran-Wernerian economics can enable the rapid shift from coal, oil and gas based CO_2-releasing energy generation to sustainable sources.

5 Conclusions The widespread despair produced by neoclassical economics can be replaced by the innovative hope of Shimomuran-Wernerian economics. Governments everywhere can do much better by making the necessary changes and practising an economics which has a proven track record in producing the goods. Neoclassical economics doesn't produce the goods—it's just a minor political economics which advantages pre-existing wealth and privilege, and is popular with the advantaged elites who think that's all that is required, but is profoundly unpopular with the voters in all democratic countries.

Shimomuran-Wernerian macroeconomics is a proven path to future prosperity for the whole human race, because

- For the people, it offers a proven growth path to much higher prosperity and is a more positive macroeconomics because it makes the most of personal inventions and factory floor innovations to produce more widely distributed wealth for the benefit of all working people
- For governments, it frees governments from funding investment only from domestic or foreign savings by providing a third way —no-cost investment credit creation—to fund much higher investment (and as Shimomura has pointed out, these additional investment funds can run at 10% to 15% of GDP for decades),
- For the less developed countries, it explains and provides a proven path (on which the Tokyo Consensus economies have already travelled) for the rapid achievement of the prosperity of their people within a few decades

- For academics, it is an intellectually satisfying macroeconomic system which is vastly superior (because it is realistically founded) than the past-its-shelf-life neoclassical macroeconomics.
- For the world, it offers a quicker and affordable way to reach a sustainable environmental balance and could minimise and reverse the rise in greenhouse gases.

In my view no better macroeconomic option is available."

****

Most Western economists do not begin to appreciate the enormous significance of Shimomuran-Wernerian macoeconomics. That fresh-to-the-west understanding has already produced four economic miracles, where four previously poor Asian countries - the nations of the Tokyo Consensus Zone, the countries of Japan, South Korea, Taiwan and China - have rapidly grown to economic greatness through that better understanding and competent governments. The way is clear for any other country with a competent government and a skilled people - and most countries could have the former, and many have the latter - to grow rapidly by adopting the Tokyo Consensus understandings set out above. I think that development has become inevitable, and a better day is dawning in most of the countries of the world.

So be it.

Appendix 2 - List of Six Books and sources of 112 Articles written or co-authored by the author of this book

Note: The author tried to advise the Thatcher governments about these issues, lobbying parliament through the Grylls Group during the 1979-83 years, but he failed to have any positive effect due to well-funded Clearing Bank opposition to the interests of the British people.

Macmillan Academic (now Palgrave Macmillan) during the 1979 to 1987 years published four books dealing with this topic as follows:

1 John C Carrington and George T Edwards, *Financing Industrial Investment*, London, Macmillan, 1979.

2 John C Carrington and George Edwards, *Reversing Economic Decline*, London, Macmillan, 1981.

3 George T Edwards, *How Economic Growth and Inflation Happen*, London, Macmillan, 1984.

4 George T Edwards, *The Role of Banks in Economic Development, The Economics of Industrial Resurgence* (Foreword by Harold Lever) Macmillan, London, 1987.

A fifth recently published book is "Shimomuran Economics and the Rise of the Tokyo Consensus" available at http://www.lulu.com/shop/george-tait-edwards/shimomuran-economics/paperback/product-21715259.html. As the cover of that book says: "The Japanese acknowledge that Dr Osamu Shimomura is their most influential post-war economist but his works and his "economic model of Japan" with its key modification of the Keynesian investment-saving equilibrium condition to create an exploding economy, seems to be virtually unknown in the economics departments of Western universities. This book traces the timeline of the development of Investment Credit Creation economics - the economic understanding which has produced explosive economic growth - from its apparent origins in FDR's USA during 1938-44 through the adoption of almost identical measures in post war Japan, with the active involvement of Dr Osamu Shimomura, and then the transfer of that new system to post-rapprochement China after 1972. In the view of the author, the Tokyo Consensus nations - China, Japan, South Korea and Taiwan - are using and continue to use the mindset of Shimomuran Economics to achieve great economic advantages and the West now needs to learn what part of Asia knows."

A sixth book is "Lucky Bastards of the 20th Century - The Story of the Economic Bomb" available at http://www.lulu.com/shop/george-tait-edwards/lucky-bastards-of-the-20th-century/paperback/product-21958236.html. The blurb about that book says

"This book sets out the creation and spread of the new economic technology of explosive economic development from its beginnings in Frank Delano Roosevelt's USA from 1938-1944 and its subsequent adoption by Japan from 1946-1985 and its spread to the China sea economies of South Korea, Taiwan and China. The book also covers the reaction of British politicians, businessmen and bankers to this new development and the circumstances around the adoption of the neoclassical economics which is resulting in the continual relative failure of the Western economies. This book sets out a more useful economics which is currently being practiced by all of the China Sea economies."

The author has also co-authored 18 articles during the 1976-85 years (eight with John Carrington, four with Harold Lever, and six on his own) on related topics in various national newspapers and magazines, during the last 40 years. These are:

2.1 John C Carrington and George T Edwards, *Where Finance Fails Investment*,
Management Today, February 1976, pp52-3,112.
2.2 John C Carrington and George T Edwards, *Britain and Japan - Is the difference the cost of capital?* The Times, 16 July 1976, p19.
2.3 John C Carrington and George T Edwards, *How Finance Fuels Growth*, Management Today June 1979, p95-6.
2.4 George T Edwards, *Could the British follow Japan's investment lead?* The Times.
2.5 John C Carrington and George T Edwards, *Let's give supply management a try,* The Guardian, 24 October 1979, p18.

2.6 John C Carrington and George T Edwards, *Keynesians and Monetarists - Are they really poles apart?* The Times 4 December 1979, p19.

2.7 Harold Lever and George Edwards, *How Germany Beats Britain,* The Sunday Times, 2 November 1980, centre pages and following page.

2.8 Harold Lever and George Edwards, *How to bank on Britain,* The Sunday Times, 9 November 1980, p16.

2.9 Harold Lever and George Edwards, *Put businessmen at head of money queue,* The Sunday Times, 7 December 1980, p19.

2.10 John C Carrington and George T Edwards, *Keynesians and Monetarists - Are they really poles apart?* The Times 4 December 1979, p19.

2.11 George T Edwards and John C Carrington, *This is the time for giving and getting credit where it's due,* The Guardian, 25 February 1981, p20.2.12 John C Carrington and George T Edwards, *A yen for greater honourable debt,* The Accountant, 24 April 1981.

2.13 Harold Lever and George Edwards, *How the Japanese make money work,* The Times, 31 July 1981, p12.

2.14 George Edwards, *Why listening to a bank's reply matters,* Guardian, 2 October 1982, p16.

2.15 George Edwards, *Bleeding to Death,* The New Democrat, July 1983, p26.

2.16 George Edwards, *Investment Projects and Profitability; the Tragic Delusion,*
Accountancy, February 1985, p131.

2.17 George Edwards, *Mrs Thatcher's Ghost Dance,* New Statesman, 24 May 1985.

2.18 George T Edwards, *Why banks have failed industry,* Your Business, September 1985, pp13-14.

There is also a total of 94 published articles authored or co-authored on the internet - 34 published on the London Progressive Journal at http://londonprogressivejournal.com/user/view/2285, ten articles co-authored with Bryan Gould at http://londonprogressivejournal.com/user/view/6214 , and fifty articles published at https://medium.com/me/stories/public.

Printed in Poland
by Amazon Fulfillment
Poland Sp. z o.o., Wrocław